FOR ORGANS, PIANOS & ELECTRONIC KEYBOARDS

E-Z PLAY® TODAY

228

SONGS OF THE 70's

THE DECADE SERIES

Y0-AGK-413

E-Z Play TODAY chord notation is designed for playing **standard chord positions** or **single key chords** on all **major brand organs** and **electronic keyboards.**

HAL•LEONARD™
CORPORATION

7777 W. BLUEMOUND RD. P.O. BOX 13819 MILWAUKEE, WI 53213

Contents

The Twenties

by Stanley Green

The Seattle Daily Times

SEATTLE, WASHINGTON, SUNDAY MORNING, MAY 22, 1927.

LINDBERGH IN PARIS!
50,000 CHEER U. S. FLYER

*I*t began with the crisp martial blare of soldiers returning home from World War I and ended with the mournful wail of the Wall Street debacle. In between, the Roaring Twenties were the years of F. Scott Fitzgerald novels and John Held Jr. cartoons, of Silent Cal in the White House and Lucky Lindy winging his lonely way across the Atlantic, of Man o' War on the turf and Rudolph Valentino, Mary Pickford, Douglas Fairbanks, Charlie Chaplin, and Rin-Tin-Tin on the silver screen. It was a period dominated by the noble experiment known as Prohibition, which may have failed to enforce alcoholic temperence but which did succeed in fostering bootlegging, speakeasies, moonshining, and mob violence personified by the menacing figure of Al Capone. It had sports heroes dubbed the Manassa Mauler, the Sultan of Swat, and the Galloping Ghost, and it offered a variety of fads and fashions, as flappers bobbed their hair and raised their skirts, and lounge lizards sported raccoon coats and baggy pants, strummed ukuleles and banjos, and drank from hip flasks. It was, in short, the period that columnist Westbrook Pegler called "the era of wonderful nonsense."

Another name for it was The Jazz Age, though the term was used less as a musical designation than to describe the decade's revolt against traditional, morals and mores. Just as the spontaneous sound of jazz broke loose from the more accepted musical forms of the past, so the spontaneous reaction to the bloody war that had just ended — and as an expression of the nation's carefree spirit during a period of economic growth — was to turn many away from long-held strictures of behavior. Thus it was only right that jazz should add the beat, the contagious ragtime meter to the mainstream of popular music as it filled the demand of a high-stepping, uninhibited society.

The optimistic spirit of the decade was neatly summed up in a bit of quack psychotherapy propounded by Dr. Emile Coué — "Day by day, in every way, I'm getting better and better." Not only did people feel that their lives could be improved by simplistic autosuggestion, there was a general attitude — expressed in the popular songs of the day — that unhappiness was only temporary and that any setback could be easily overcome. We were told that April showers bring May flowers. That there would be no more sobbin' when the red, red robin comes bob, bob, bobbin' along. That when you're smiling, the whole world smiles at you. That all you need on a rainy day is to let a smile be your umbrella.

It should also be noted that most of the so-called jazz songs of the period were more razzmatazz than real jazz. Still, there was no question that the syncopated beat was much in evidence in such infectious pieces as "Baby Face," "Five Foot Two, Eyes of Blue," and "Everybody Loves My Baby." Some numbers even addressed themselves directly to the new rhythm, such as "Crazy Rhythm," which offered the observation, "What's the use of Prohibition? You produce the same condition." There was, however, a more authentic jazz sound in the songs written and performed by black writers and entertainers. In 1929, Louis Armstrong took over Fats Waller's "Ain't Misbehavin'" when he was appearing in the Broadway show *Hot Chocolates* and turned it into a trademark number. Ethel Waters did the same for "There'll Be Some Changes Made," one of her earliest recordings. And the black vaudeville team of Henry Creamer and Turner Layton introduced their own tribute to the cradle of jazz, "'Way Down Yonder In New Orleans."

Since jazz was king in the Twenties, there had to be a King of Jazz. Ever since first arriving in New York in 1920 to appear at the Palais Royale nightclub, the undisputed crown-wearer was a rotund orchestra leader named Paul Whiteman. Whiteman's brand of orchestral — even symphonic — jazz may not have been for the purists, but it did help to popularize the form as well as to elevate the entire field of American dance music. Among the Whiteman specialties were such numbers as the blues novelty "Wang Wang Blues," the romantic "In A Little Spanish Town," the dreaming "Among My Souvenirs," and the Fats Waller-Andy Razaf "Honeysuckle Rose." Another song, the foot-stomping "Mississippi Mud," was more than an orchestra specialty, since it also served to introduce audiences to a vocal trio known as the Rhythm Boys, one of whom was a 24-year-old crooner from Tacoma named Bing Crosby.

Paul Whiteman and his Orchestra

Rhythm Boys

The Twenties also saw the emergence of other topflight bands that introduced and popularized many of the lasting hits of the decade. "'Deed I Do" was identified with the "Ol' Maestro" Ben Bernie ("Yowzah, yowzah"), while "Me And My Shadow," "When My Sugar Walks Down The Street," "Star Dust," and "Sugar Blues" were associated with, respectively, Ted Lewis, Phil Harris, Isham Jones, and Clyde McCoy. In 1929, crooning idol Rudy Vallee fronted a dance band known as the Connecticut Yankees and turned a thirteen-year-old English ballad, "If You Were The Only Girl In The World," into a hit in the United States.

The Song Favorite of the KING and QUEEN of England
GOOD NIGHT SWEETHEART
by
RAY NOBLE
JIMMY CAMPBELL
& REG CONNELLY
American Version by
RUDY VALLEE

Introduced in America
by
RUDY VALLEE

Also featured in
EARL CARROLL VANITIES
(9th Edition)

ROBBINS MUSIC CORPORATION New York
by arrangement with
Campbell, Connelly & Co. London, Eng.

The leading entertainer of the decade was the dynamic Al Jolson, who wore blackface makeup, dropped to one knee and flung out his arms as he vowed to walk a million miles for one of his Mammy's smiles. Even in his Broadway shows, Jolson always interpolated his own specialties, such as "April Showers" and "California, Here I Come" in *Bombo* (1921), and "If You Knew Susie Like I Know Susie" and "It All Depends On You" in *Big Boy* (1925).

Al Jolson

Eddie Cantor

Probably Jolson's closest rival as a song-and-dance attraction was the energetic, eye-popping Eddie Cantor, who originally billed himself as "The Apostle of Pep." Cantor's repertory included such songs as "Ma! He's Making Eyes At Me" (sung in *The Midnight Rounders*), "Baby Face," and "If You Knew Susie," which though introduced by Jolson, became far more closely identified with Cantor. Another Cantor specialty, "Yes! We Have No Bananas," caused more of a sensation in the Twenties than any other novelty number. Actually, it was a patchwork song made up by stringing together five recognizable themes: the "Hallelujah" chorus from Handel's "Messiah," the last line from "My Bonnie Lies Over The Ocean," the middle part of "I Dreamt That I Dwelt In Marble Halls," the line "I was seeing Nellie home" from "Aunt Dinah's Quilting Party," and Cole Porter's "An Old Fashioned Garden."

$\mathcal{A}$ part from phonographs and Broadway shows, the chief area for introducing popular songs in the Twenties was vaudeville which, for a modest price, offered audiences variety bills consisting of just about every form of entertainment — from song-and-dance performers to acrobats, from comedy sketches to dramatic scenes, from animal acts to operatic excerpts. Among headliners of the decade were torch singer Ruth Etting (who introduced "Mean To Me"), chirpy-voiced Cliff "Ukulele Ike" Edwards ("I Cried For You" and "Paddlin' Madelin' Home"), the harmonizing duo of Van and Schenck ("Who's Sorry Now?"), the singing and dancing Duncan Sisters ("Let A Smile Be Your Umbrella" and "Side By Side"), and Sophie Tucker, billed as "The Last Of The Red Hot Mamas" ("When The Red, Red Robin Comes Bob, Bob, Bobbin' Along").

Florenz Ziegfeld

Jerome Kern

$\mathcal{U}$ nquestionably, however, it was Broadway that provided the most prestigious outlet for the most glittering stars and the most accomplished composers and lyricists. It was also the domain of the legendary Florenz Ziegfeld, who presided over seven editions of his celebrated *Follies* revue during the decade. Especially notable was the 1921 production in which comedienne Fanny Brice introduced the seriocomic lament "Second Hand Rose." Ziegfeld also sponsored two major book shows of the Twenties: Jerome Kern's *Sally* starring Marilyn Miller (who sang the memorable "Look For The Silver Lining") and another Kern musical, the classic *Show Boat*, written with Oscar Hammerstein II (whence came the tender "Make Believe" and the powerful "Ol' Man River").

The Twenties were also significant for introducing many of the creative giants of the musical theatre. Richard Rodgers and Lorenz Hart enjoyed their first Broadway success in 1925 with *The Garrick Gaieties*, which included the durable "Sentimental Me" and "Manhattan." Composer Vincent Youmans, who made his Broadway bow in 1921, wrote "Hallelujah!" for *Hit The Deck!* and "More Than You Know" for *Great Day!* Jimmy McHugh and Dorothy Fields attracted notice with their first show, *Blackbirds Of 1928*, whose most popular number was the confession of an impecunious swain, "I Can't Give You Anything But Love." And the triad of B.G. DeSylva, Lew Brown and Ray Henderson caught the spirit of the decade's flaming youth with such songs as "The Varsity Drag" in *Good News!*, "You're The Cream In My Coffee" in *Hold Everything!* and "Button Up Your Overcoat" in *Follow Thru*.

Though sound on film had been demonstrated as early as 1900 at the Paris International Exposition, the first feature-length motion pictures with a musical background score did not come along until 1926 with the release of *Don Juan*, starring John Barrymore. That was followed by another silent film with musical accompaniment, *What Price Glory*, which gave us our first theme song in Erno Rapee's "Charmaine." But the real revolution took place the next year when *The Jazz Singer* offered both the sight and the sound of Al Jolson singing and talking. In 1928, Jolson starred in a second popular vehicle, *The Singing Fool*, which found the singer belting out two of his biggest hits, "Sonny Boy" and "I'm Sitting On Top Of The World."

Richard Rodgers and Lorenz Hart

*B*ut the boom years were quickly coming to an end. The so-called "Coolidge prosperity," which continued under President Herbert Hoover, suddenly collapsed on "Black Thursday," October 24, 1929, when the stock market began its five-day plunge that resulted in the loss of over $32 billion worth of equities. By the end of the decade, the horn of plenty was empty as the nation braced itself for the most severe and protracted Depression in its history.

VARIETY 25¢

NEW YORK, WEDNESDAY, OCTOBER 30, 1929

WALL ST. LAYS AN EGG

The New York Times.

Copyright, 1929, by The New York Times Company.

NEW YORK, TUESDAY, OCTOBER 29, 1929.

STOCK PRICES SLUMP $14,000,000,000 IN NATION-WIDE STAMPEDE TO UNLOAD; BANKERS TO SUPPORT MARKET TODAY

Ain't Misbehavin'

Registration 7
Rhythm: Fox Trot or Swing

Words by Andy Razaf
Music by Thomas Waller and Harry Brooks

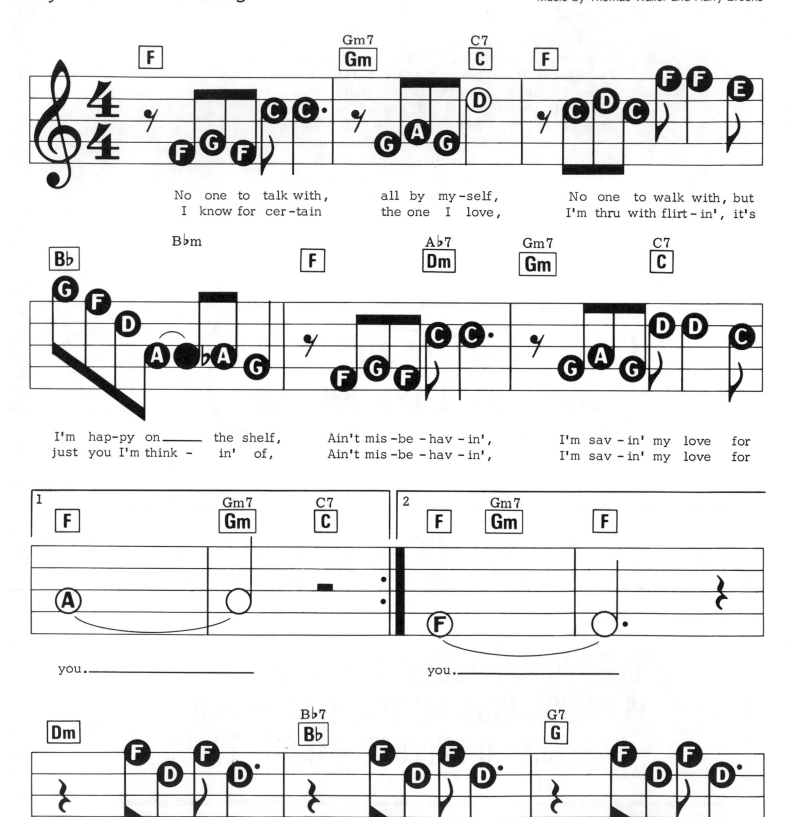

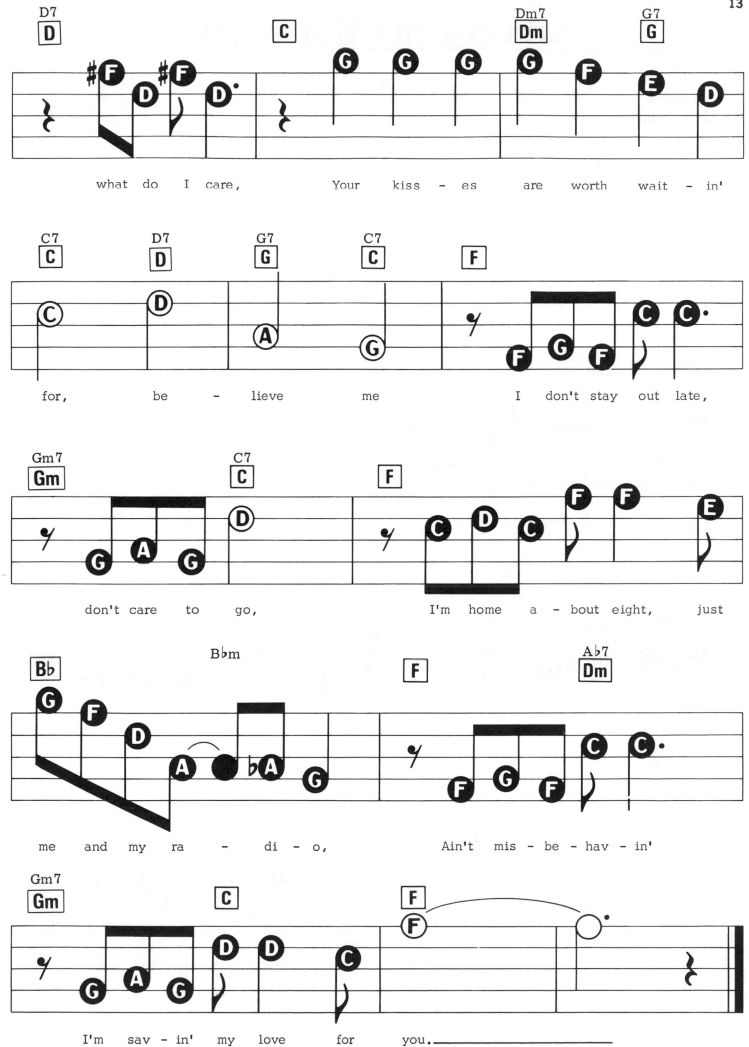

Among My Souvenirs

Registration 9
Rhythm: Swing

Words by Edgar Leslie
Music by Horatio Nicholls

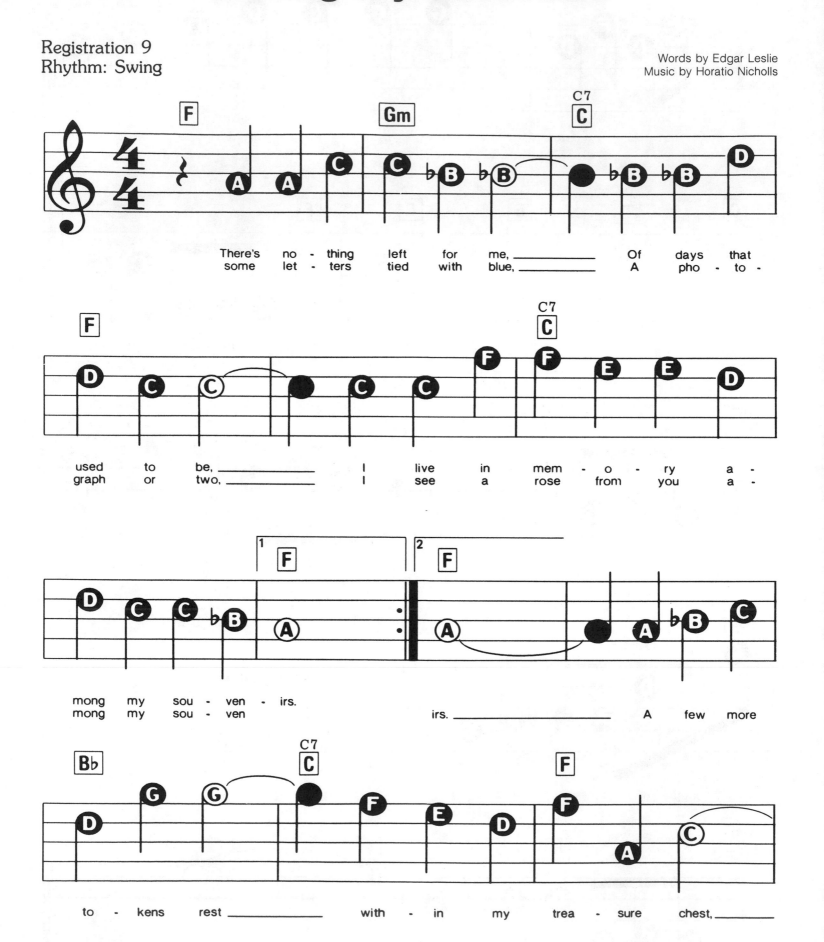

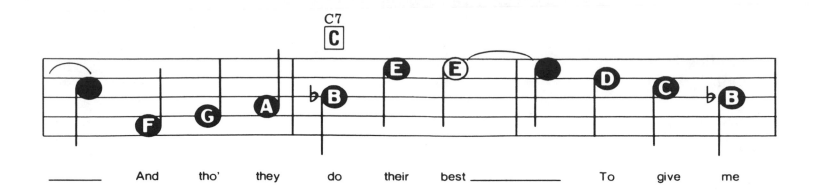

And tho' they do their best _____ To give me

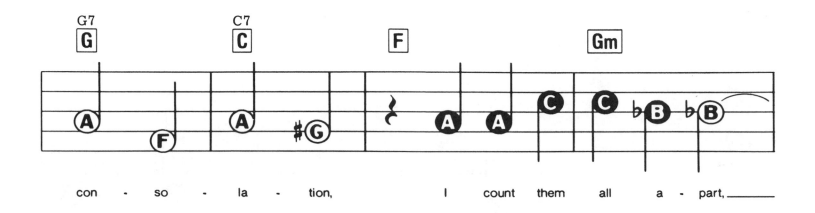

con - so - la - tion, I count them all a - part, _____

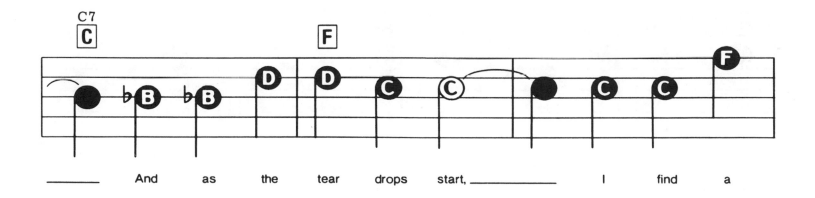

_____ And as the tear drops start, _____ I find a

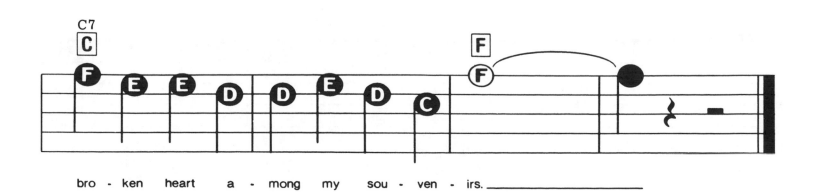

bro - ken heart a - mong my sou - ven - irs. _____

April Showers

Registration 9
Rhythm: Fox Trot

Words by B.G. DeSylva
Music by Louis Silvers

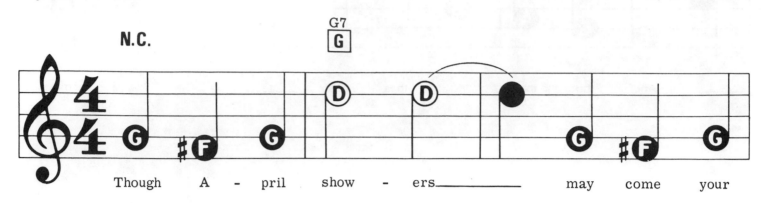

Though A - pril show - ers_____ may come your

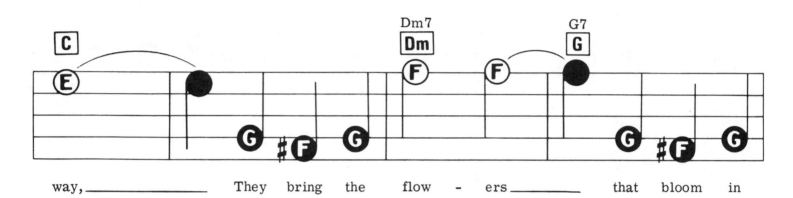

way,_____ They bring the flow - ers_____ that bloom in

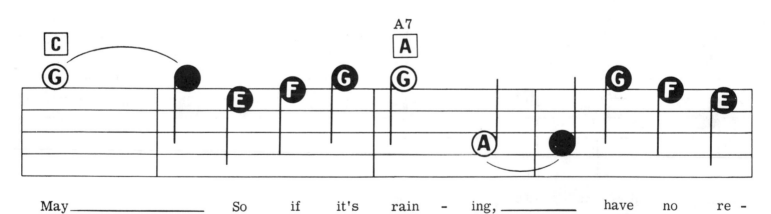

May_____ So if it's rain - ing,_____ have no re -

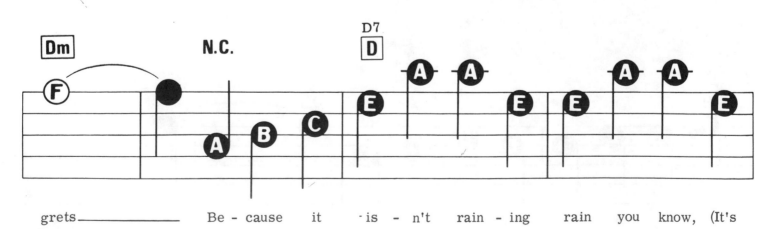

grets_____ Be - cause it is - n't rain - ing rain you know, (It's

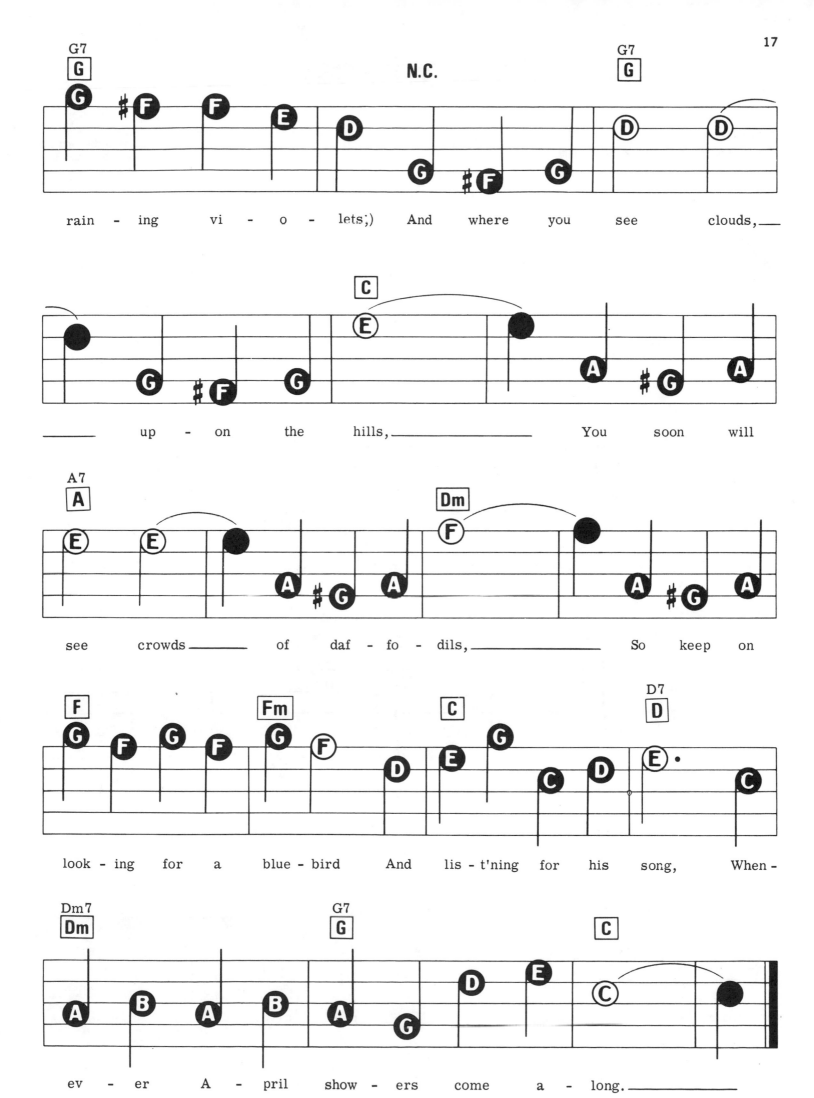

Baby Face

Registration 9
Rhythm: Fox Trot or Swing

Words and Music by
Benny Davis and Harry Akst

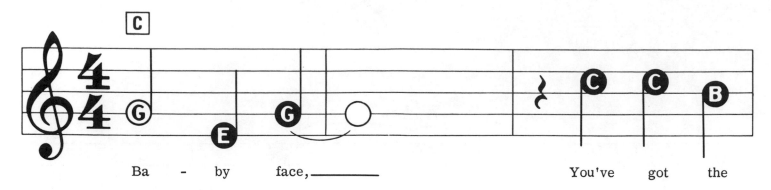

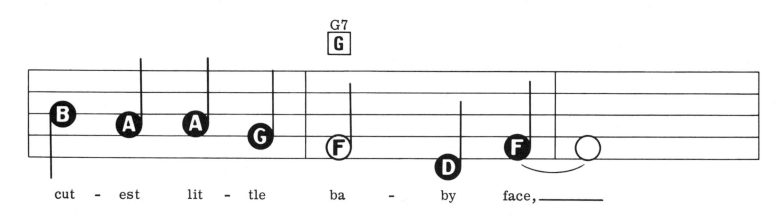

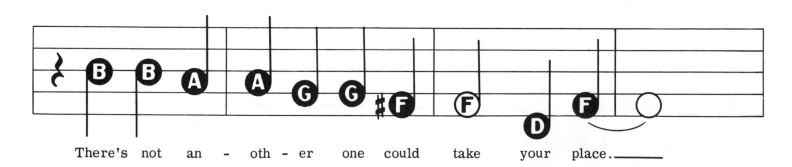

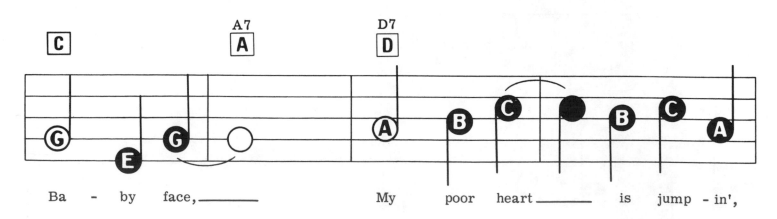

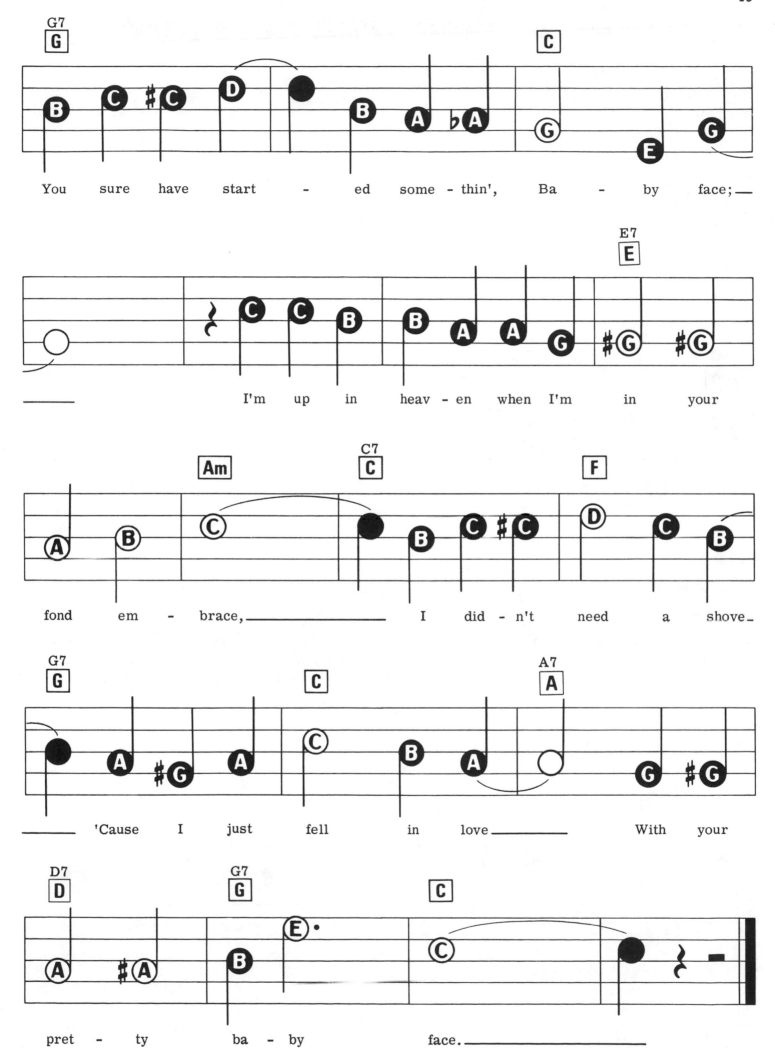

Back In Your Own Backyard

Registration 10
Rhythm: Swing

Words and Music by Al Jolson,
Billy Rose and Dave Dreyer

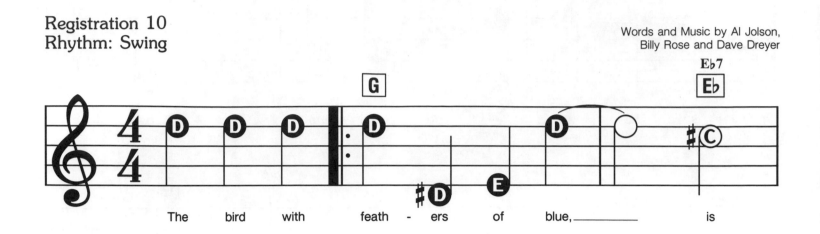

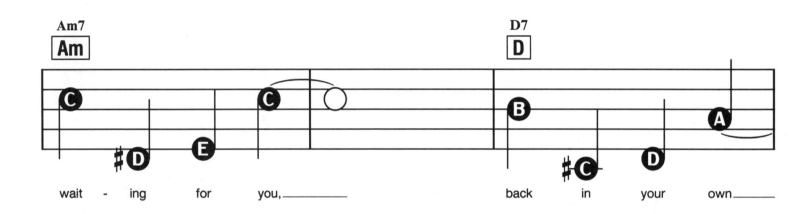

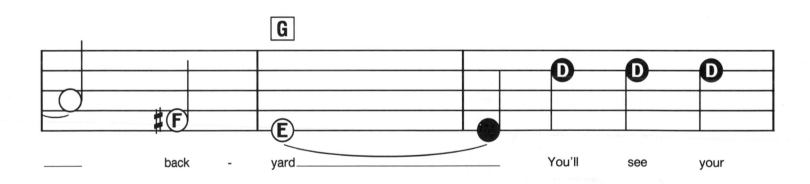

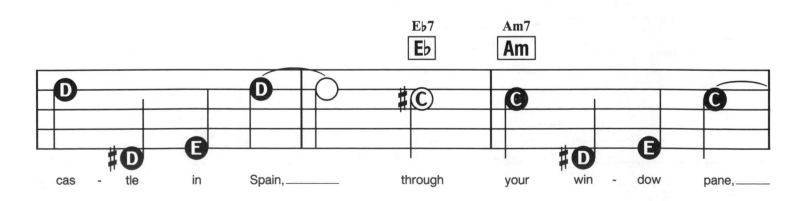

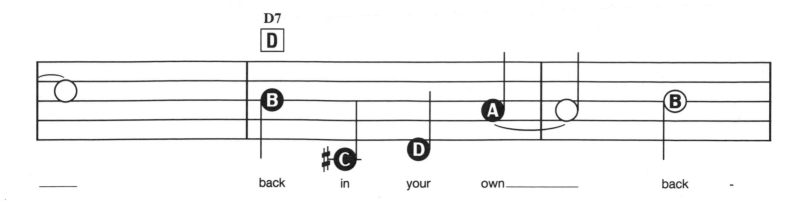

back in your own_____ back -

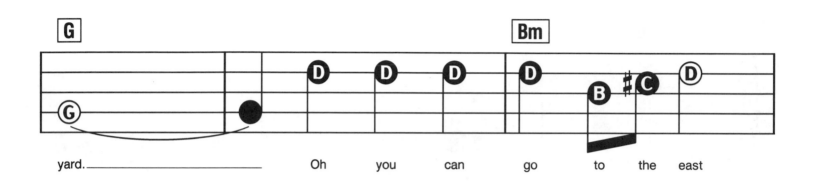

yard._____ Oh you can go to the east

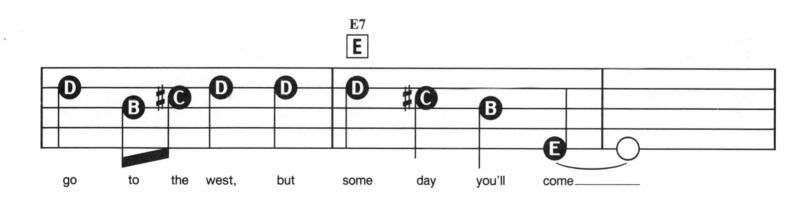

go to the west, but some day you'll come_____

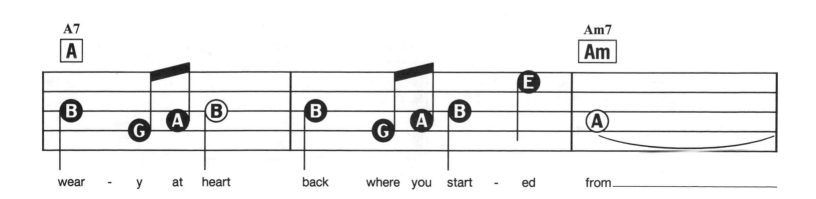

wear - y at heart back where you start - ed from_____

22

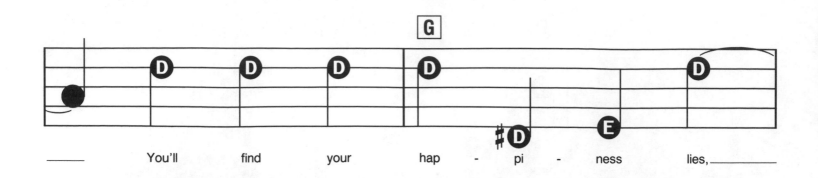

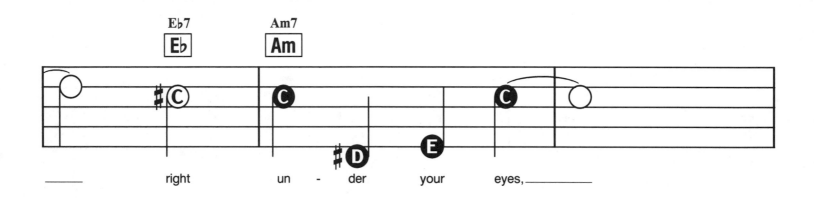

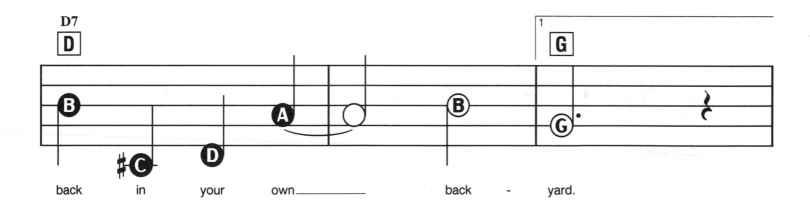

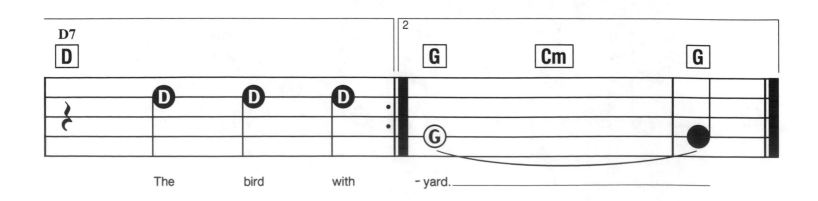

I Can't Believe That You're In Love With Me

Registration 9
Rhythm: Swing

Words and Music by
Jimmy McHugh and Clarence Gaskill

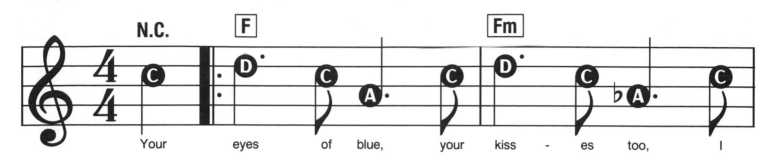

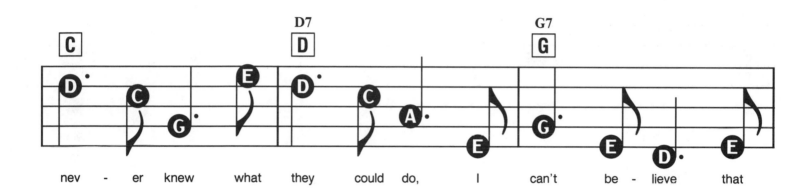

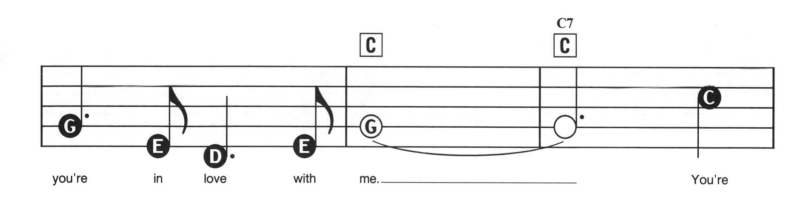

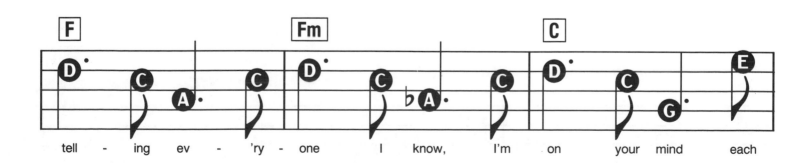

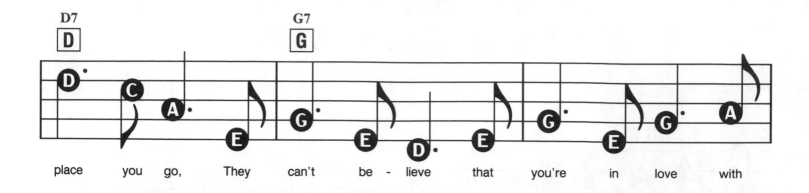

place you go, They can't be - lieve that you're in love with

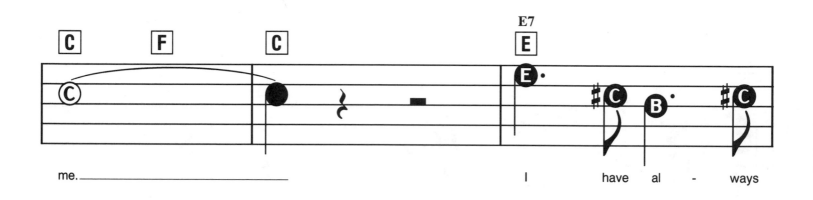

me. I have al - ways

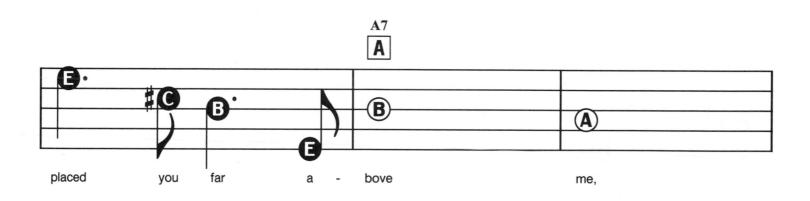

placed you far a - bove me,

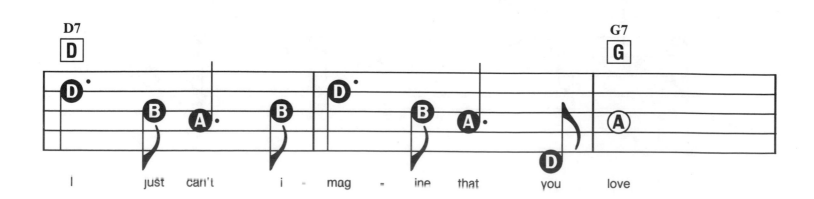

I just can't i - mag - ine that you love

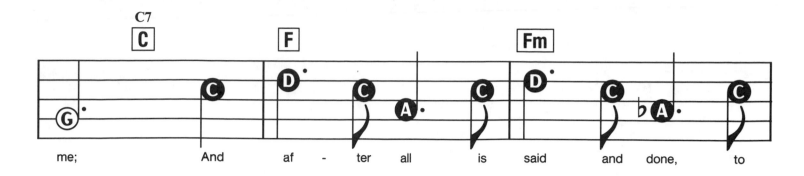

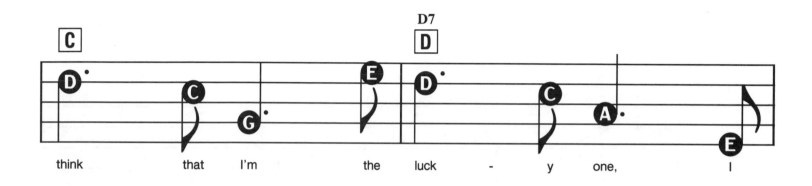

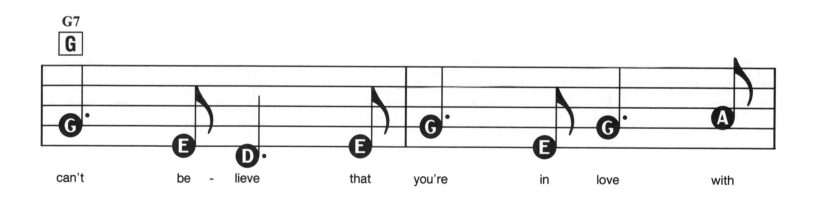

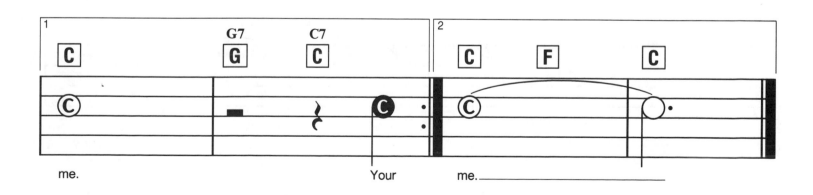

The Best Things In Life Are Free

(From "GOOD NEWS!")

Registration 8
Rhythm: Fox Trot or Swing

Words by B.G. DeSylva,
Lew Brown and Ray Henderson,

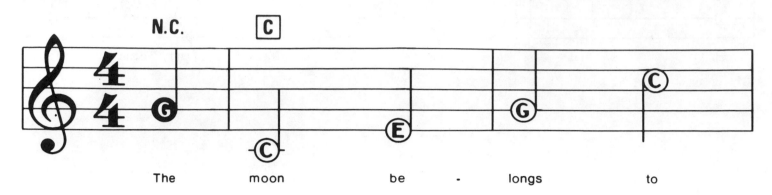

The moon be - longs to

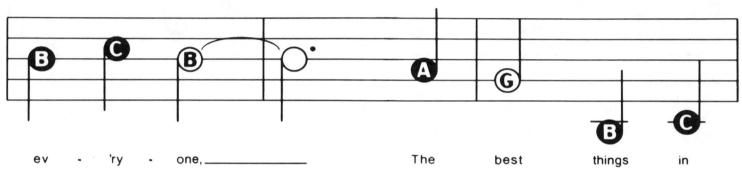

ev - 'ry - one, _____ The best things in

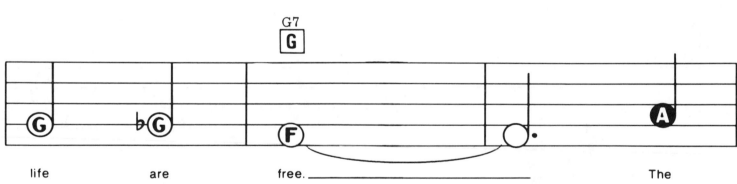

life are free. _____ The

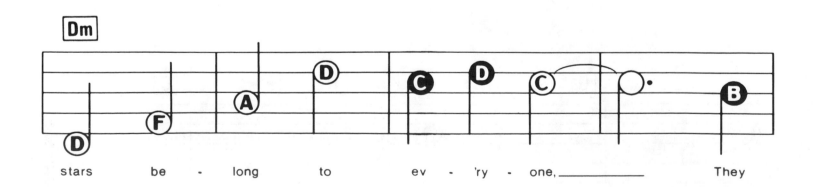

stars be - long to ev - 'ry - one, _____ They

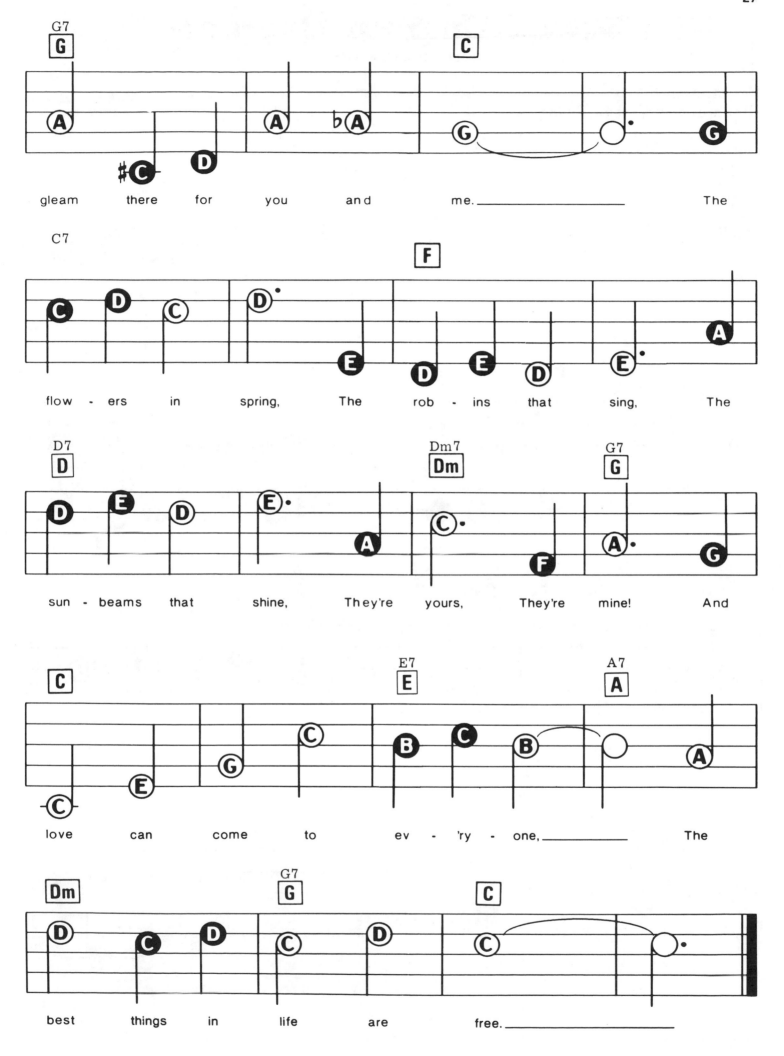

Button Up Your Overcoat

(From "FOLLOW THRU")

Registration 5
Rhythm: Fox Trot or Swing

Words and Music by B.G. DeSylva,
Lew Brown and Ray Henderson

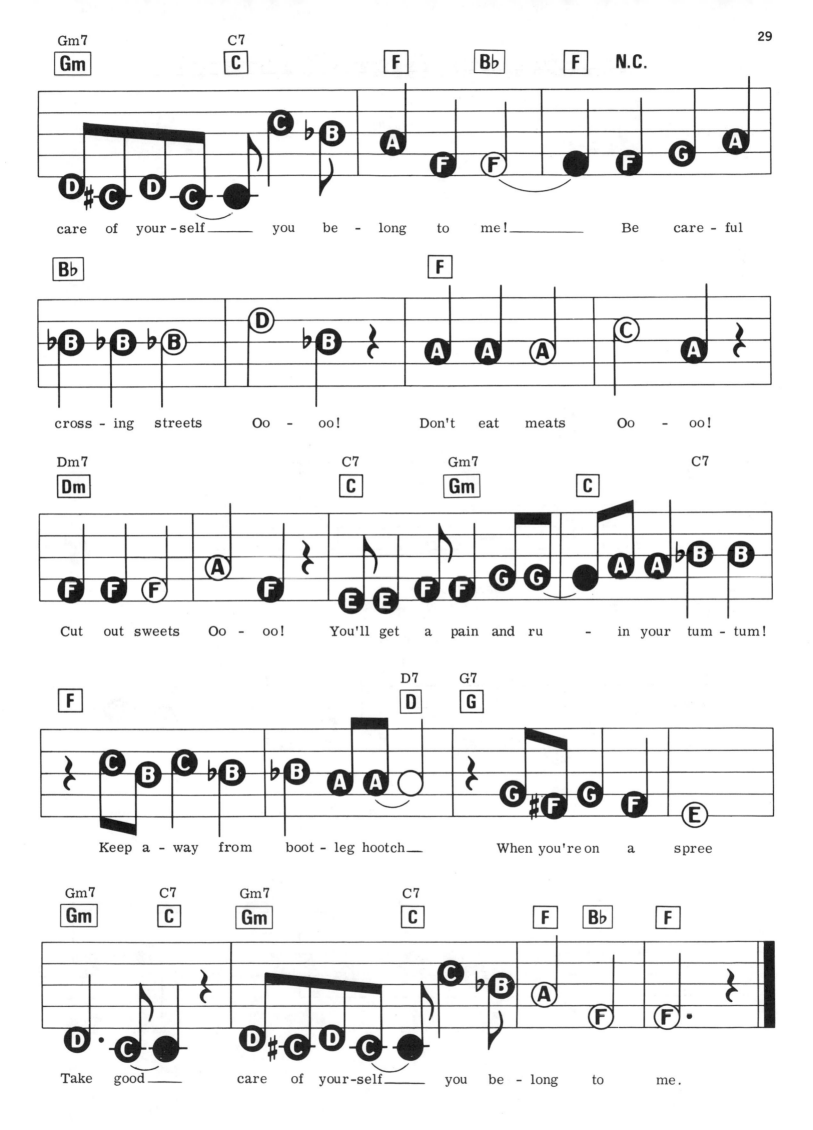

California (Here I Come)

Registration 5
Rhythm: Swing or Jazz

Words and Music by Al Jolson,
B.G. DeSylva and Joseph Meyer

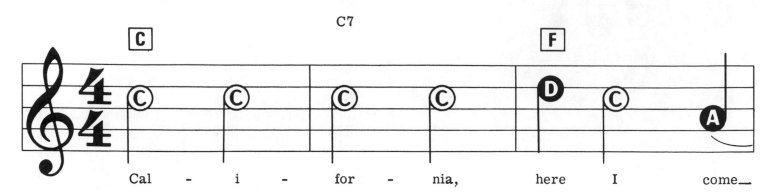

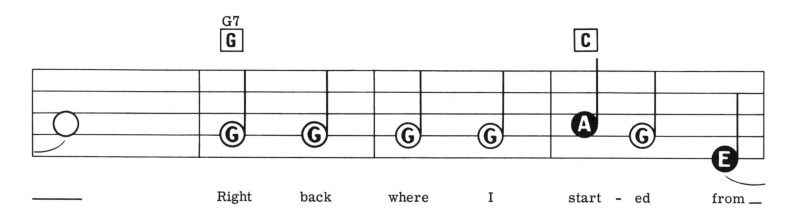

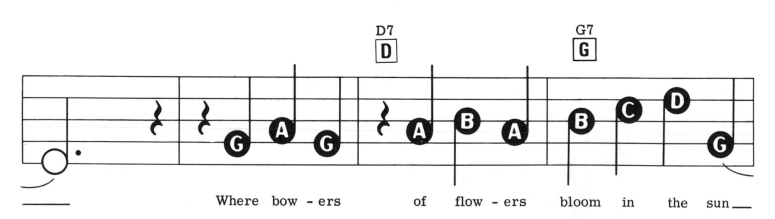

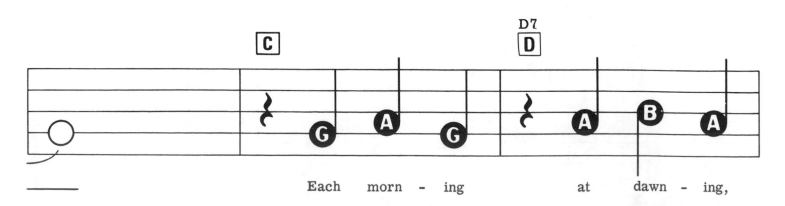

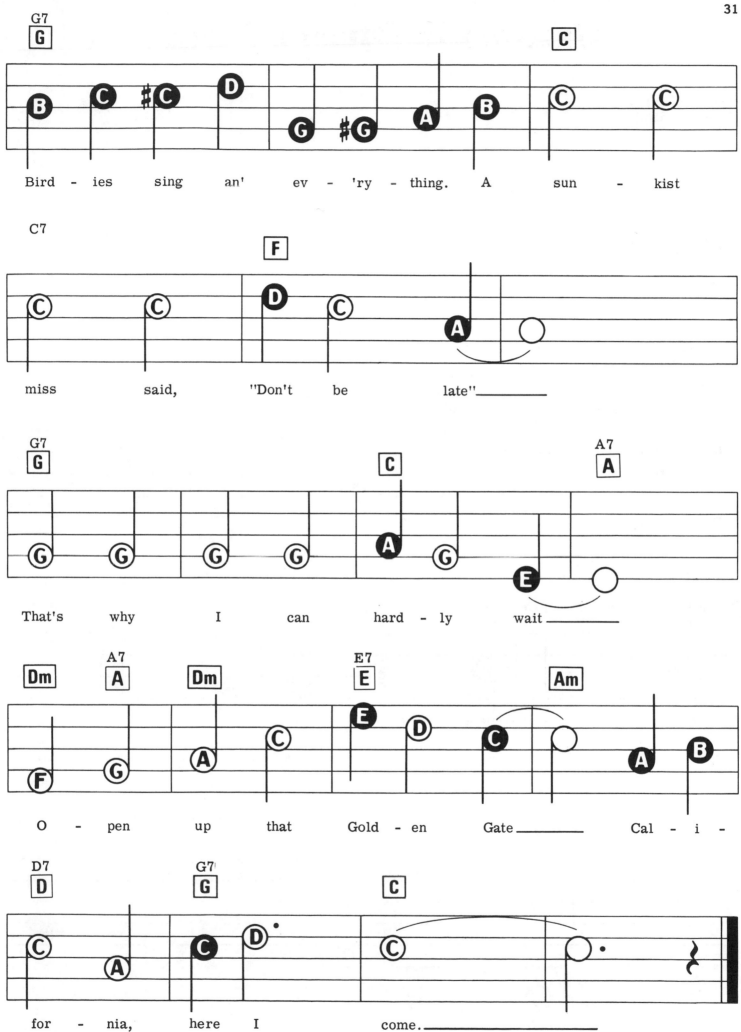

Charmaine

Registration 8
Rhythm: Waltz

Words and Music by
Lew Pollack and Erno Rapee

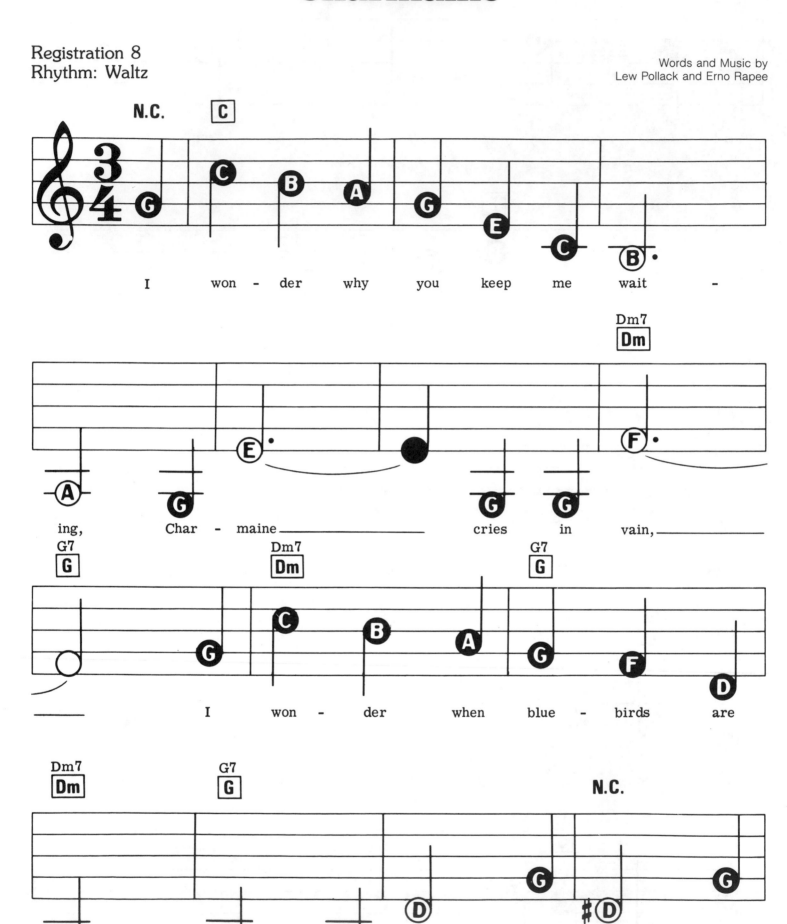

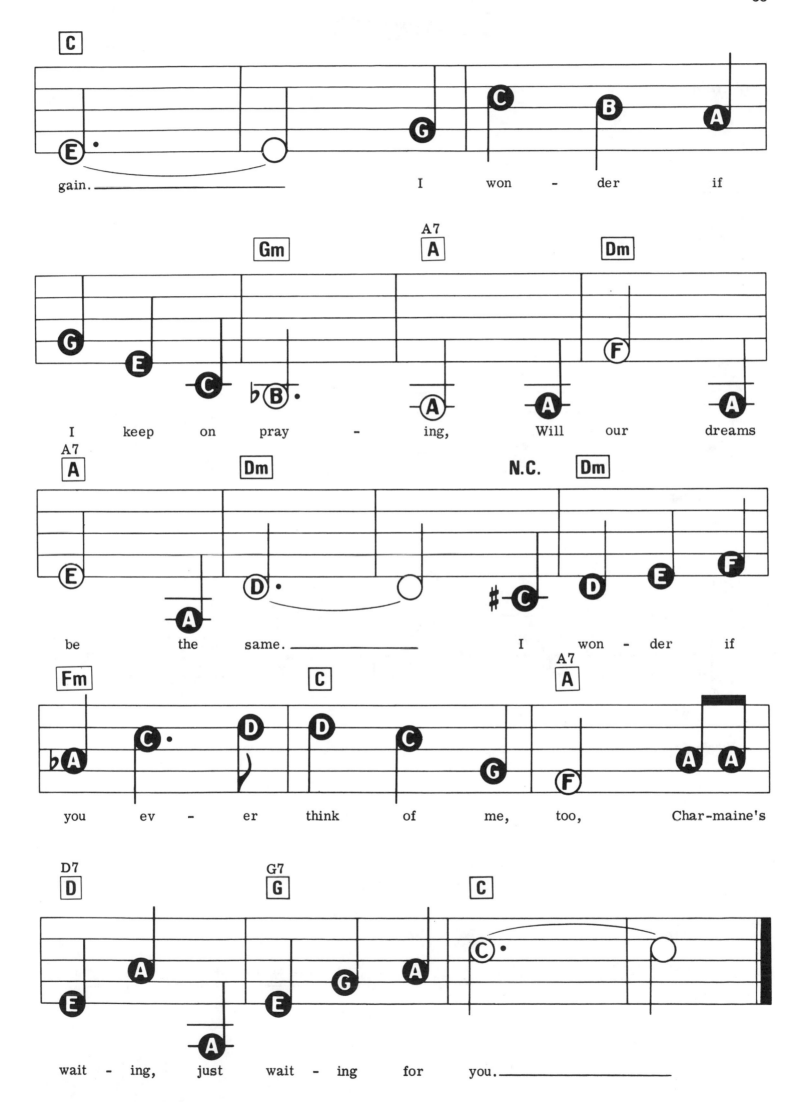

Collegiate

Registration 1
Rhythm: March

By Moe Jaffe and Nat Bonx

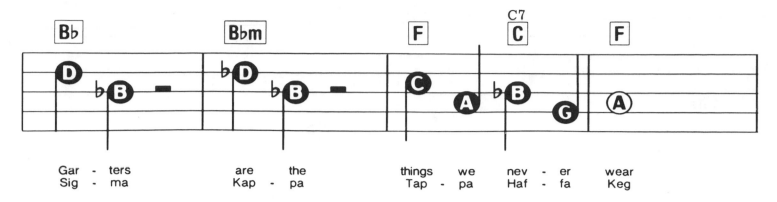

Gar - ters   are   the   things   we   nev - er   wear
Sig - ma   Kap - pa   Tap - pa   Haf - fa   Keg

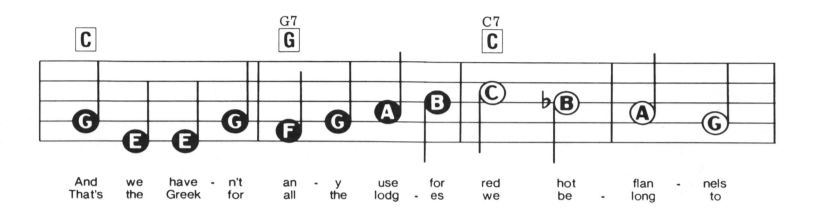

And   we   have - n't   an - y   use   for   red   hot   flan - nels
That's   the   Greek   for   all   the   lodg - es   we   be - long   to

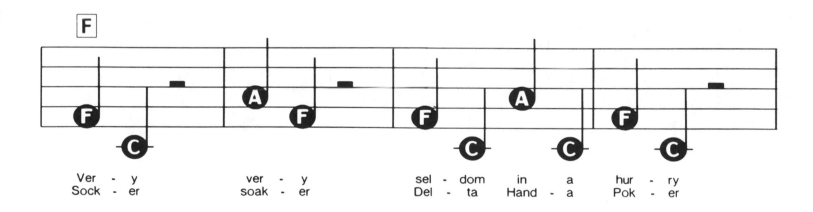

Ver - y   ver - y   sel - dom   in   a   hur - ry
Sock - er   soak - er   Del - ta   Hand - a   Pok - er

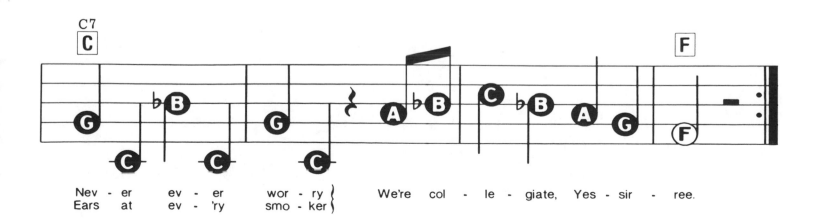

Nev - er   ev - er   wor - ry }   We're   col - le - giate, Yes - sir - ree.
Ears   at   ev - 'ry   smo - ker }

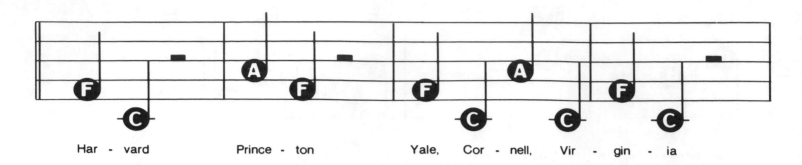

Har - vard   Prince - ton   Yale,   Cor - nell,   Vir - gin - ia

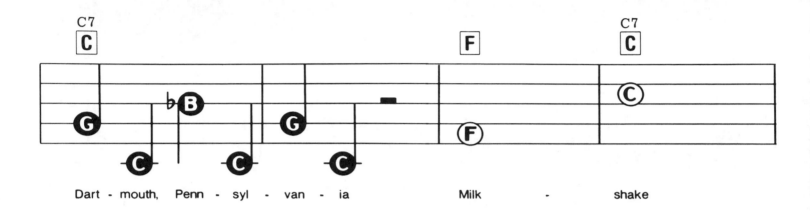

Dart - mouth,   Penn - syl - van - ia   Milk - shake

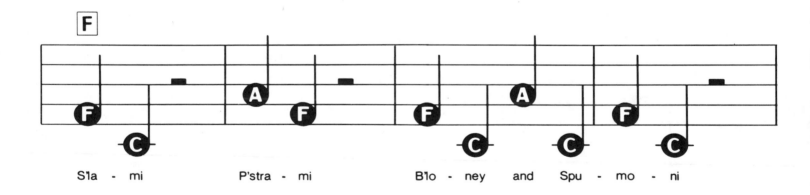

Sla - mi   P'stra - mi   Blo - ney   and   Spu - mo - ni

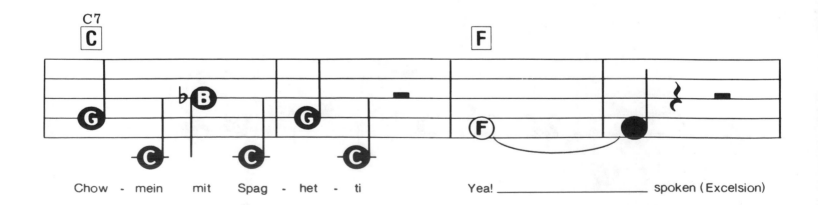

Chow - mein   mit   Spag - het - ti   Yea! _____ spoken (Excelsion)

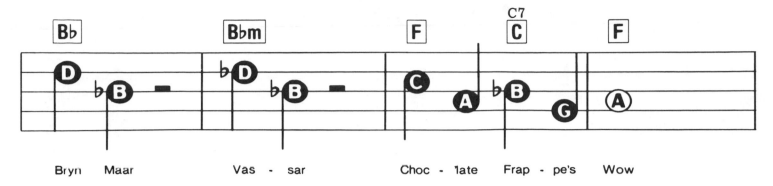

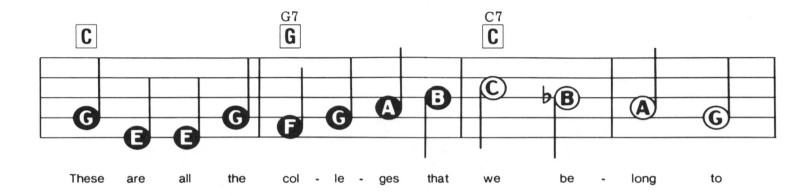

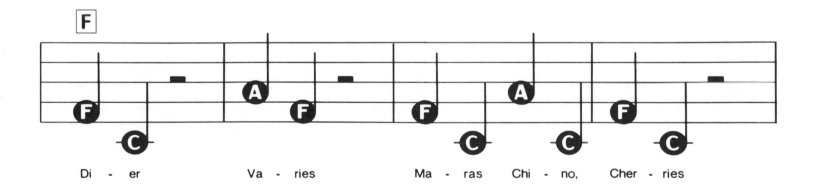

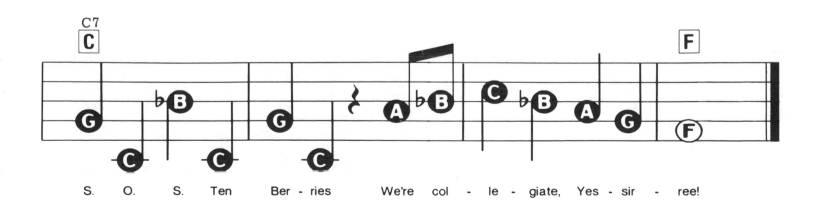

Crazy Rhythm

Registration 7
Rhythm: Swing or Jazz

Words by Irving Caesar
Music by Joseph Meyer and Roger Wolfe Kahn

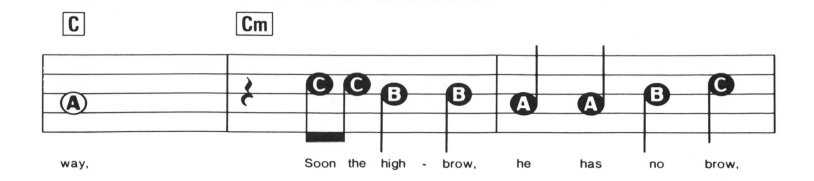

way, Soon the high - brow, he has no brow,

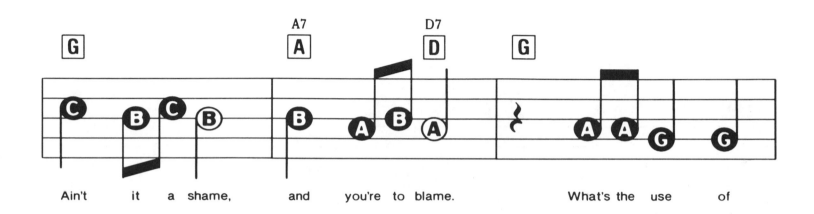

Ain't it a shame, and you're to blame. What's the use of

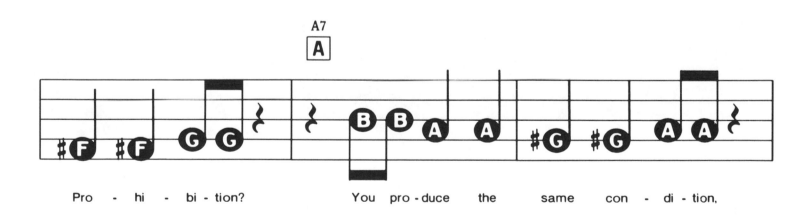

Pro - hi - bi - tion? You pro - duce the same con - di - tion,

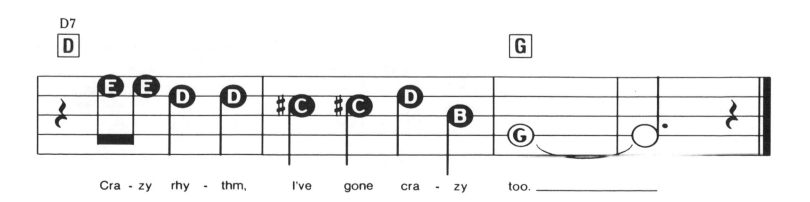

Cra - zy rhy - thm, I've gone cra - zy too. _____

'Deed I Do

Registration 2
Rhythm: Swing or Jazz

Words and Music by
Walter Hirsch and Fred Rose

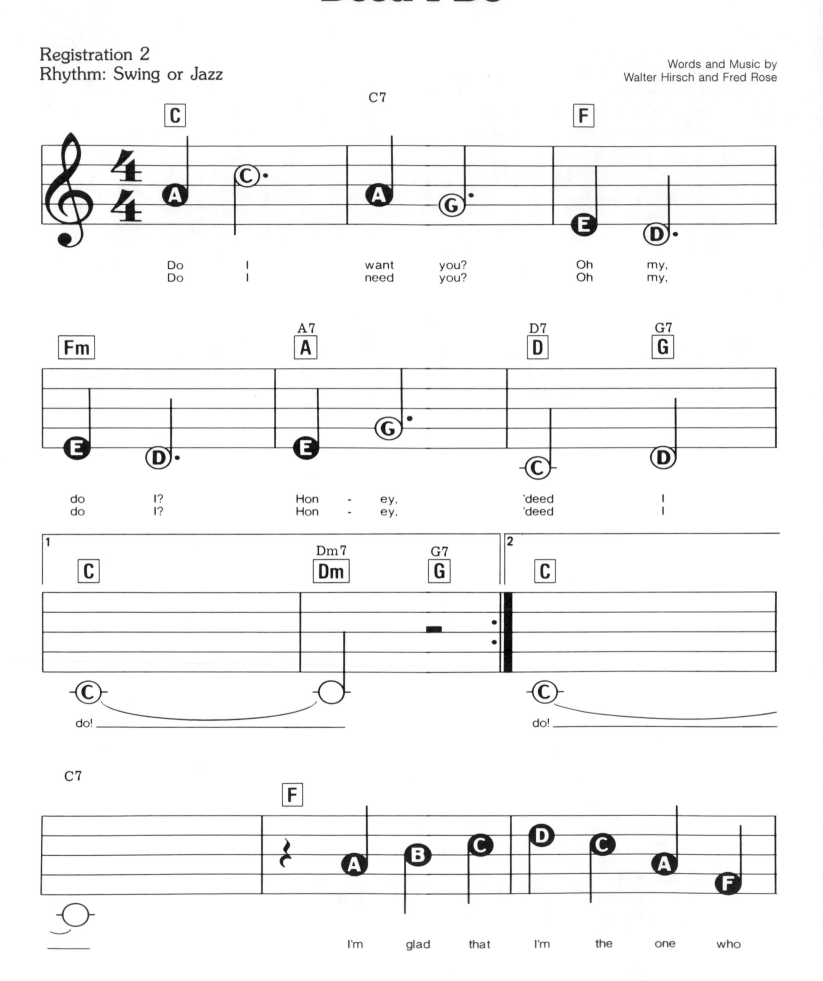

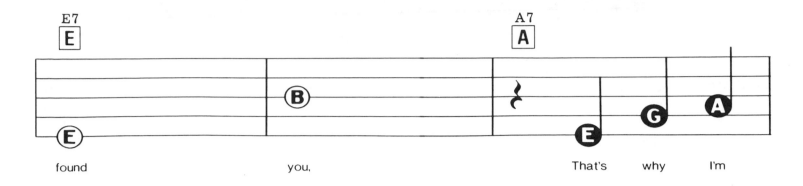

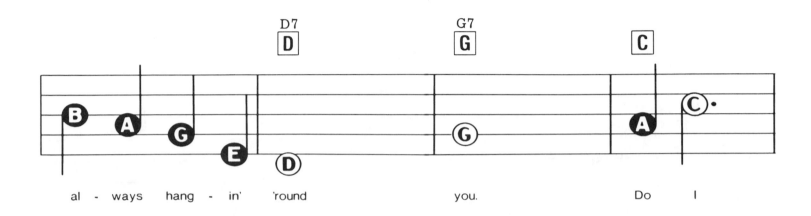

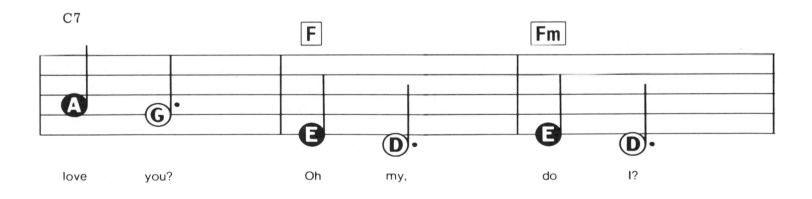

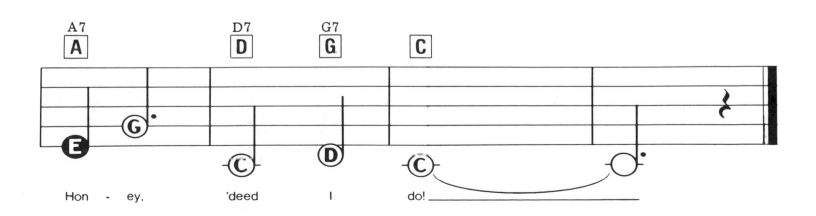

Everybody Loves My Baby
(But My Baby Don't Love Nobody But Me)

Registration 5
Rhythm: Swing or Fox Trot

Words and Music by
Jack Palmer & Spencer Williams

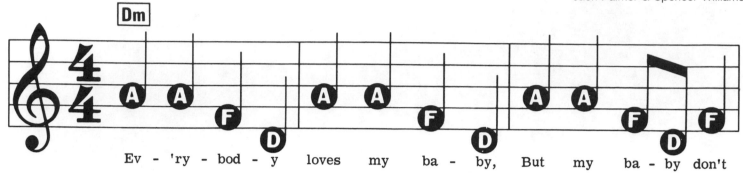

Ev - 'ry - bod - y loves my ba - by, But my ba - by don't

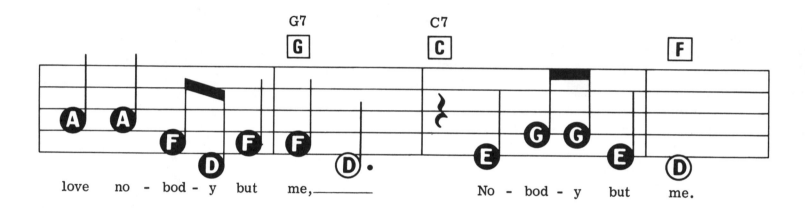

love no - bod - y but me,_____ No - bod - y but me.

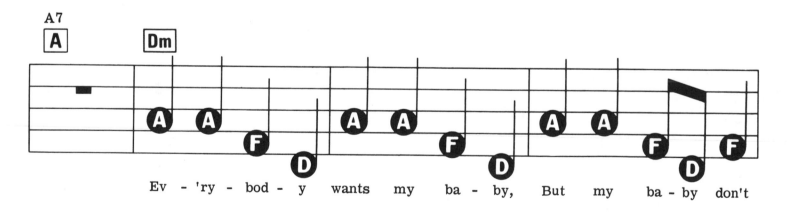

Ev - 'ry - bod - y wants my ba - by, But my ba - by don't

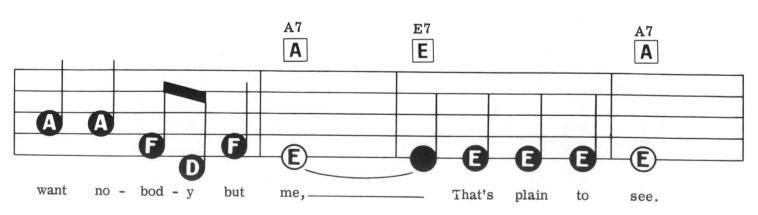

want no - bod - y but me,_____ That's plain to see.

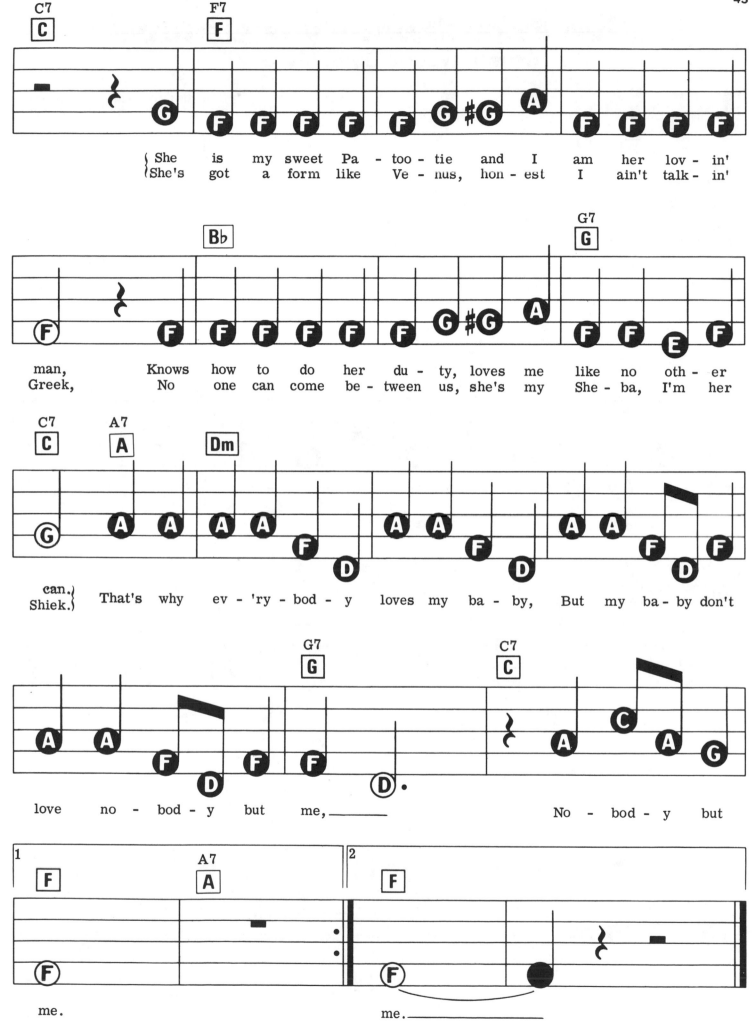

Five Foot Two, Eyes Of Blue
(Has Anybody Seen My Girl?)

Registration 9
Rhythm: Fox Trot

Words by Joe Young and Sam Lewis
Music by Ray Henderson

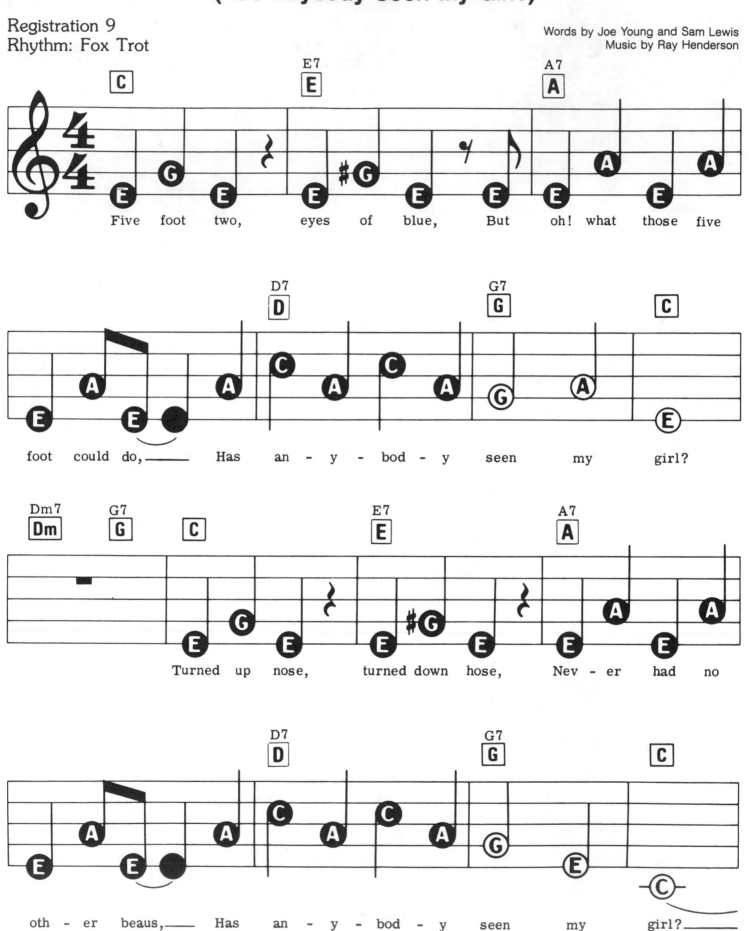

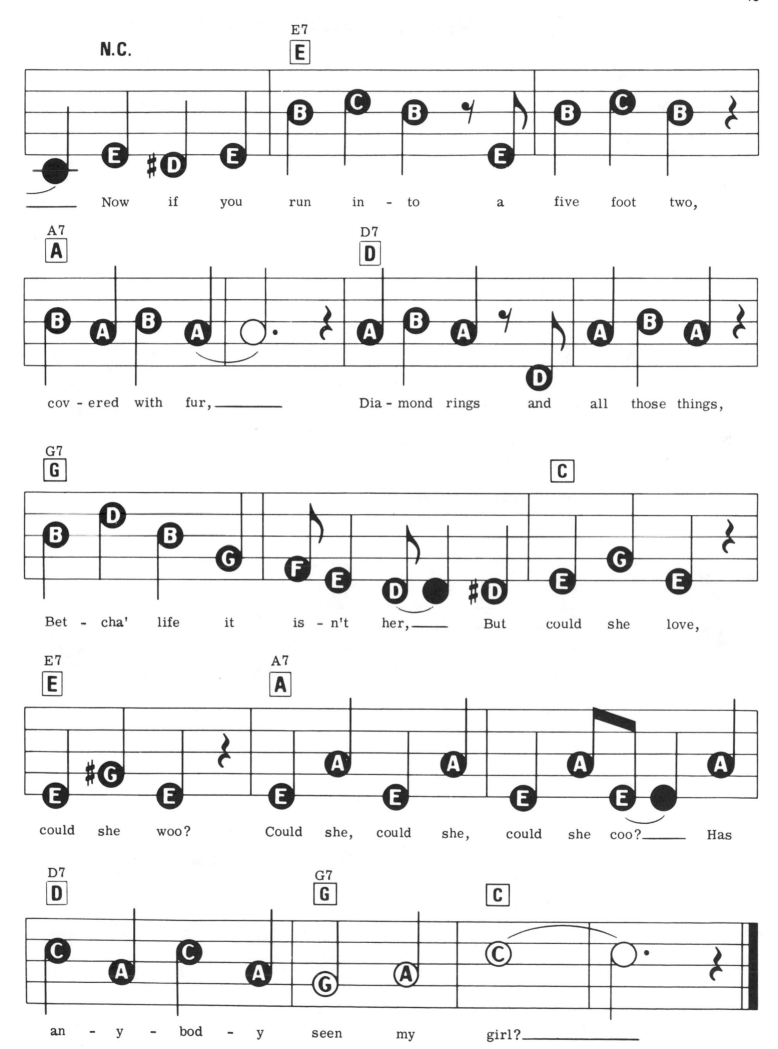

Hallelujah

Registration 7
Rhythm: Swing or Jazz

Words by Clifford Grey and Leo Robin
Music by Vincent Youmans

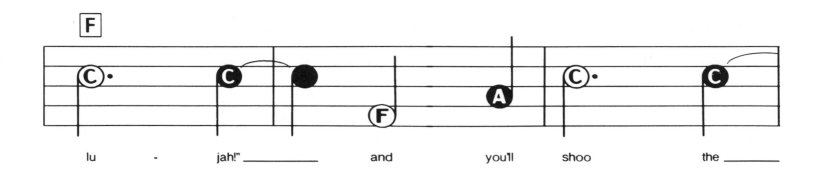

Sing "Hal - le - lu - jah! _____ Hal - le -

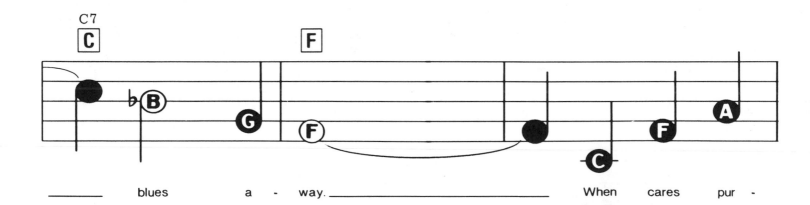

lu - jah!" _____ and you'll shoo the _____

blues a - way. _____ When cares pur -

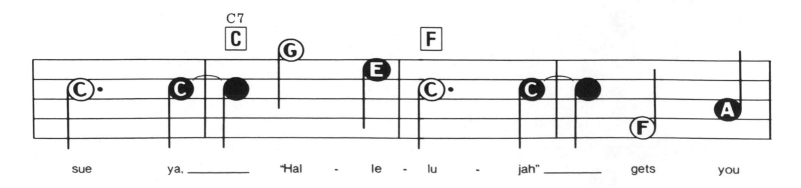

sue ya, _____ "Hal - le - lu - jah" _____ gets you

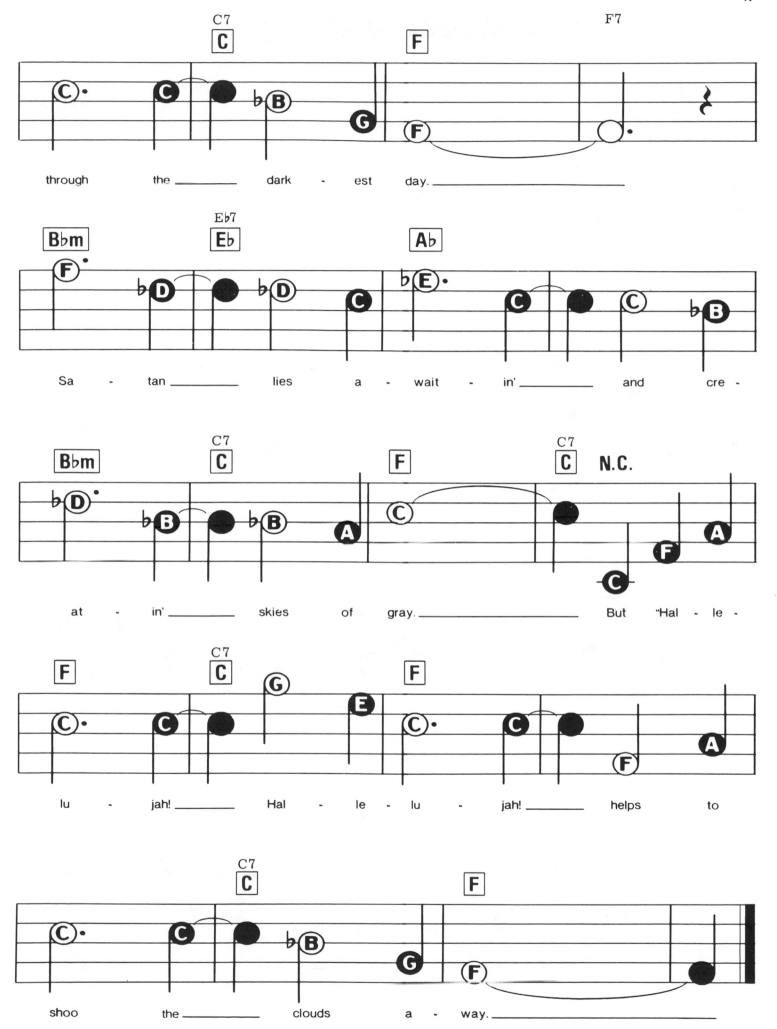

Honeysuckle Rose

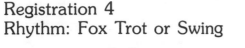

Registration 4
Rhythm: Fox Trot or Swing

Words by Andy Razaf
Music by Thomas ("Fats") Waller

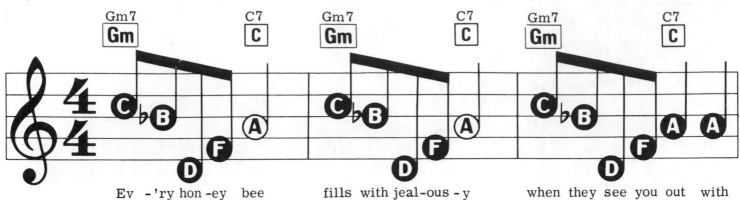

Ev-'ry hon-ey bee fills with jeal-ous-y when they see you out with

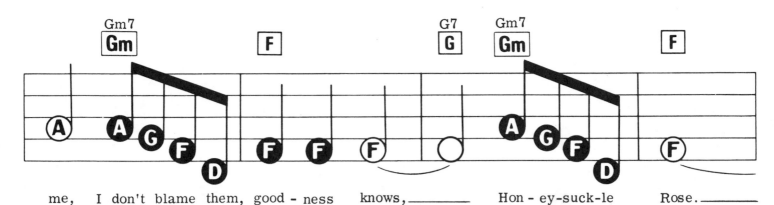

me, I don't blame them, good-ness knows,_____ Hon-ey-suck-le Rose._____

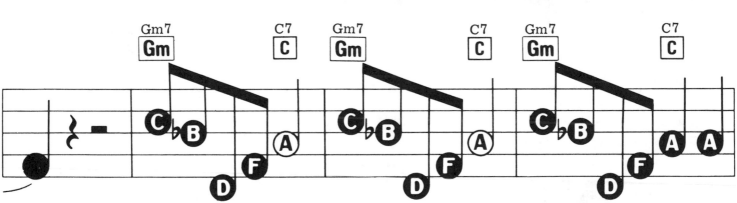

_____ When you're pass-in' by flow-ers droop and sigh, and I know the rea-son

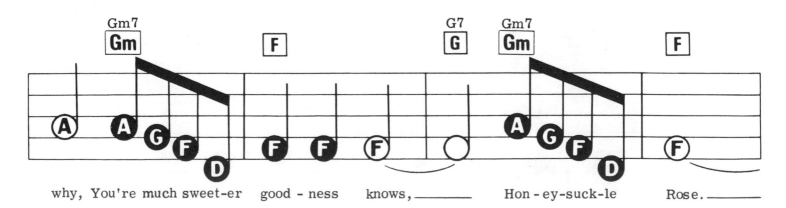

why, You're much sweet-er good-ness knows,_____ Hon-ey-suck-le Rose._____

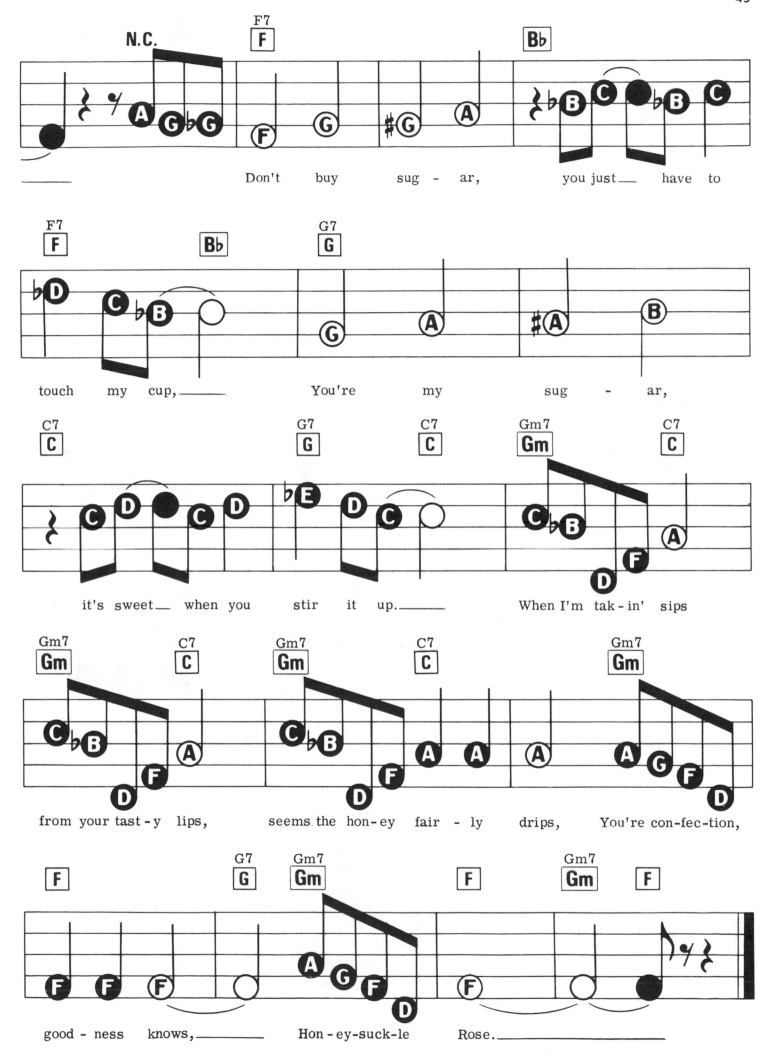

I Can't Give You Anything But Love

Registration 5
Rhythm: Swing or Jazz

Words by Dorothy Fields
Music by Jimmy McHugh

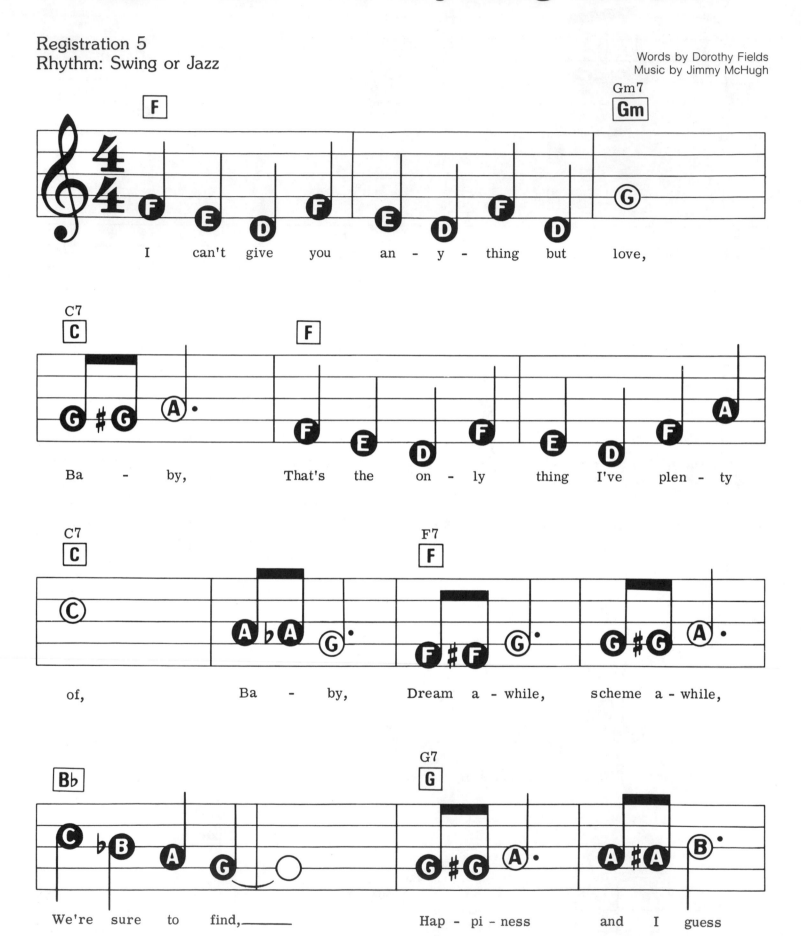

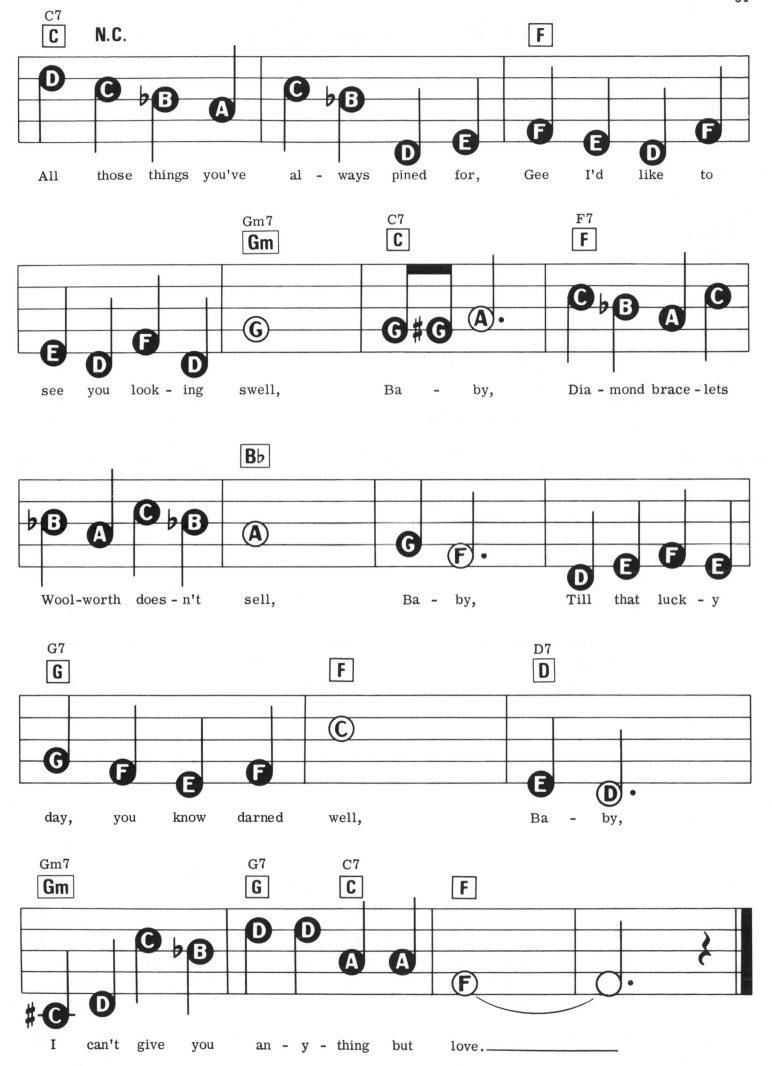

I Cried For You

Registration 2
Rhythm: Swing or Jazz

Words and Music by Arthur Freed,
Gus Arnheim and Abe Lyman

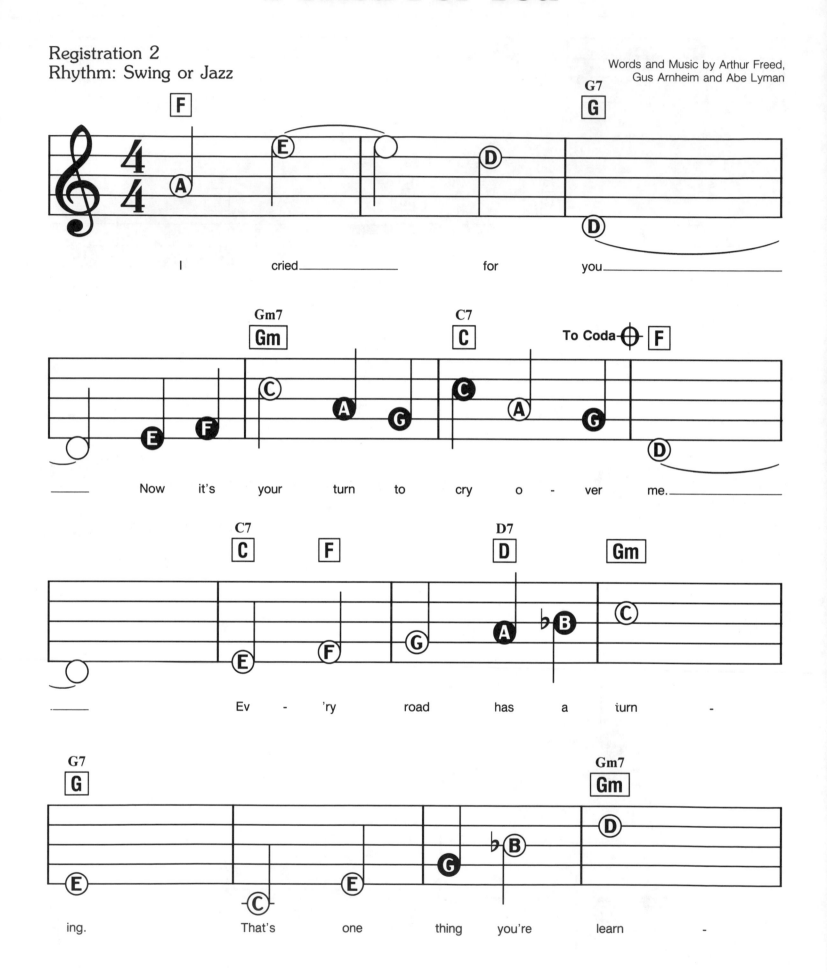

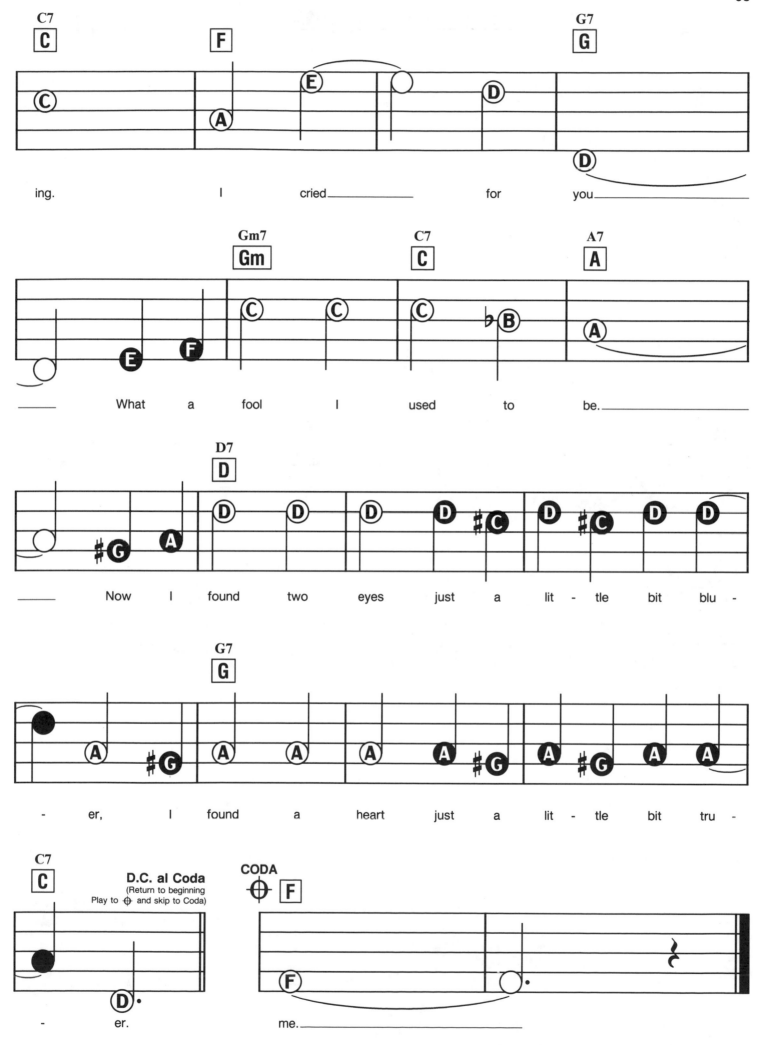

I'm Sitting On Top Of The World

(From "THE JOLSON STORY")

Registration 3
Rhythm: Fox Trot

Words by Sam M. Lewis and Joe Young
Music by Ray Henderson

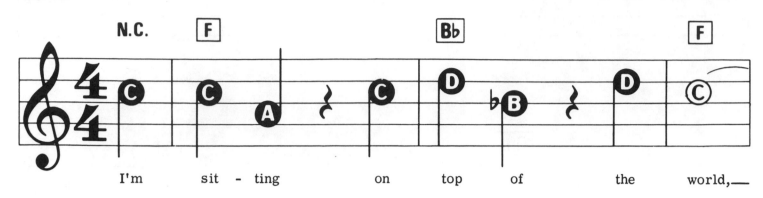

I'm sit - ting on top of the world,

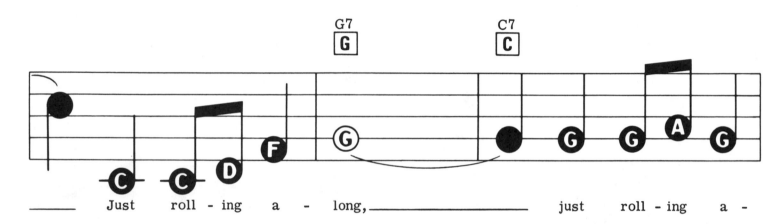

Just roll - ing a - long, just roll - ing a -

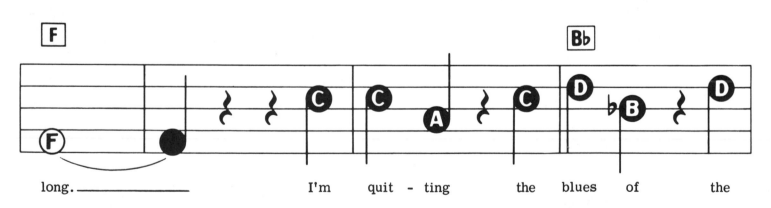

long. I'm quit - ting the blues of the

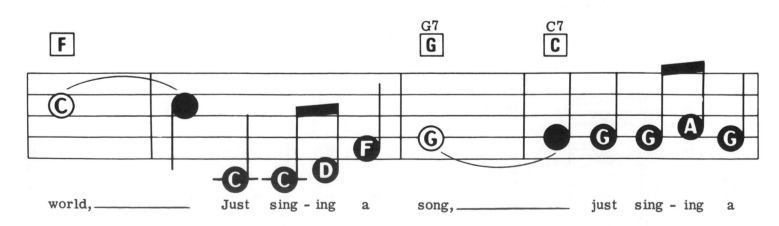

world, Just sing - ing a song, just sing - ing a

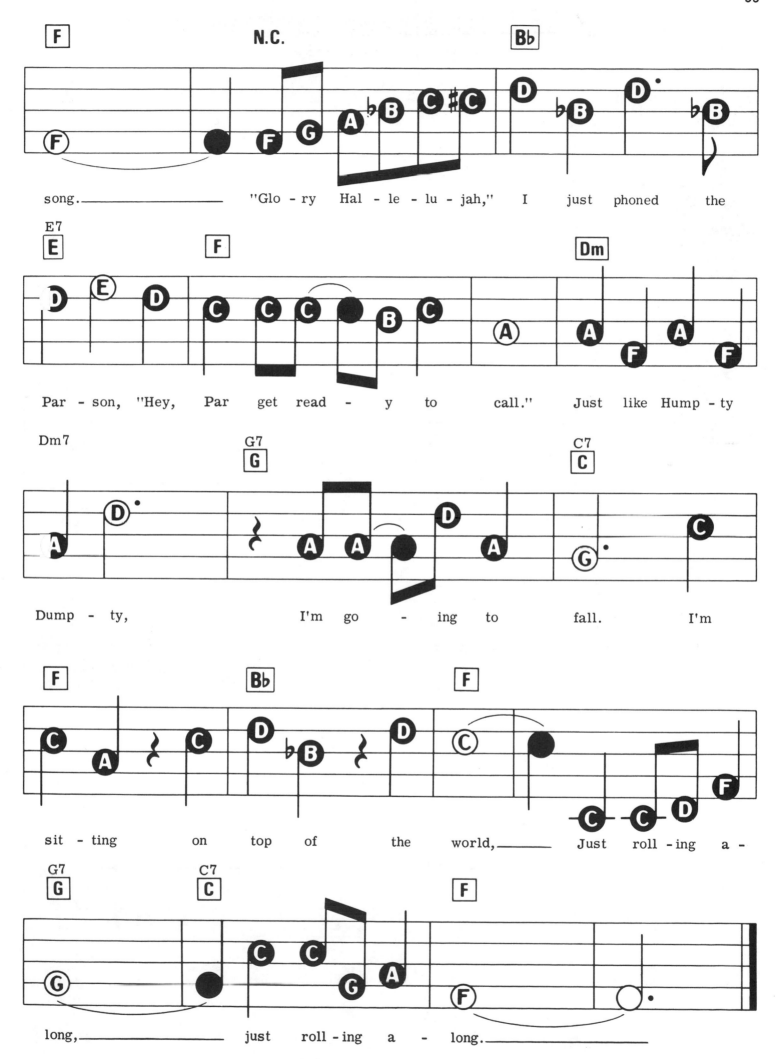

If You Knew Susie
(Like I Know Susie)

Registration 2
Rhythm: Fox Trot or March

Words and Music by
B.G. DeSylva and Joseph Meyer

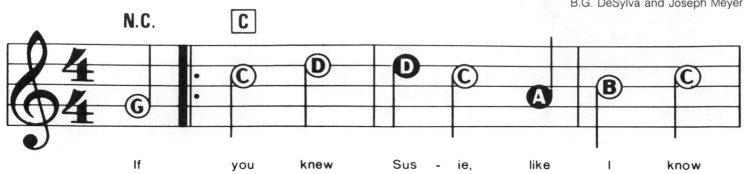

If you knew Sus - ie, like I know

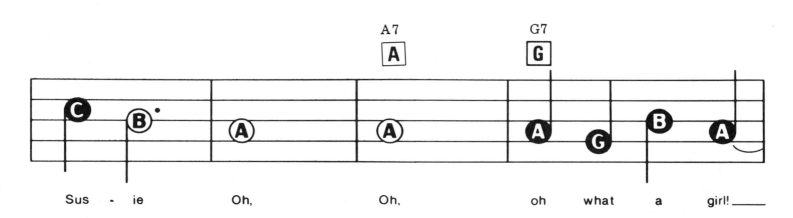

Sus - ie Oh, Oh, oh what a girl! ____

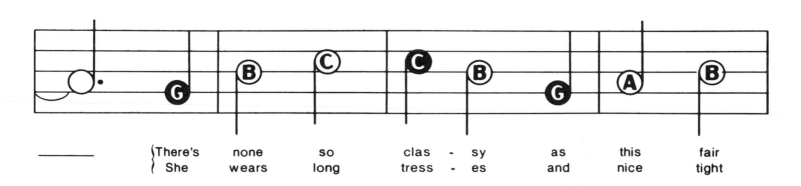

____ {There's none so clas - sy as this fair
She wears long tress - es and nice tight

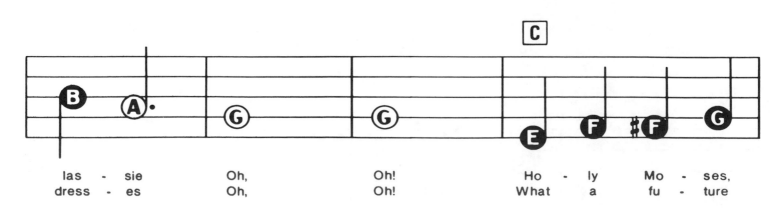

las - sie Oh, Oh! Ho - ly Mo - ses,
dress - es Oh, Oh! What a fu - ture

If You Were The Only Girl In The World

Words by Clifford Grey
Music by Nat D. Ayer

Registration 10
Rhythm: Waltz

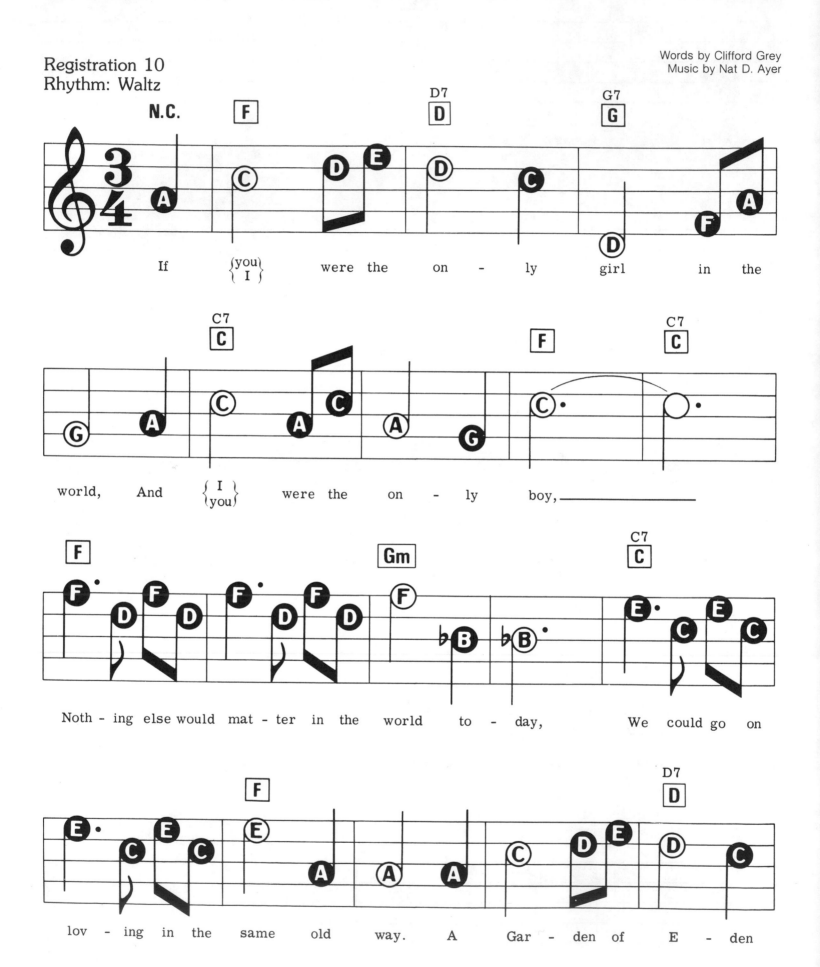

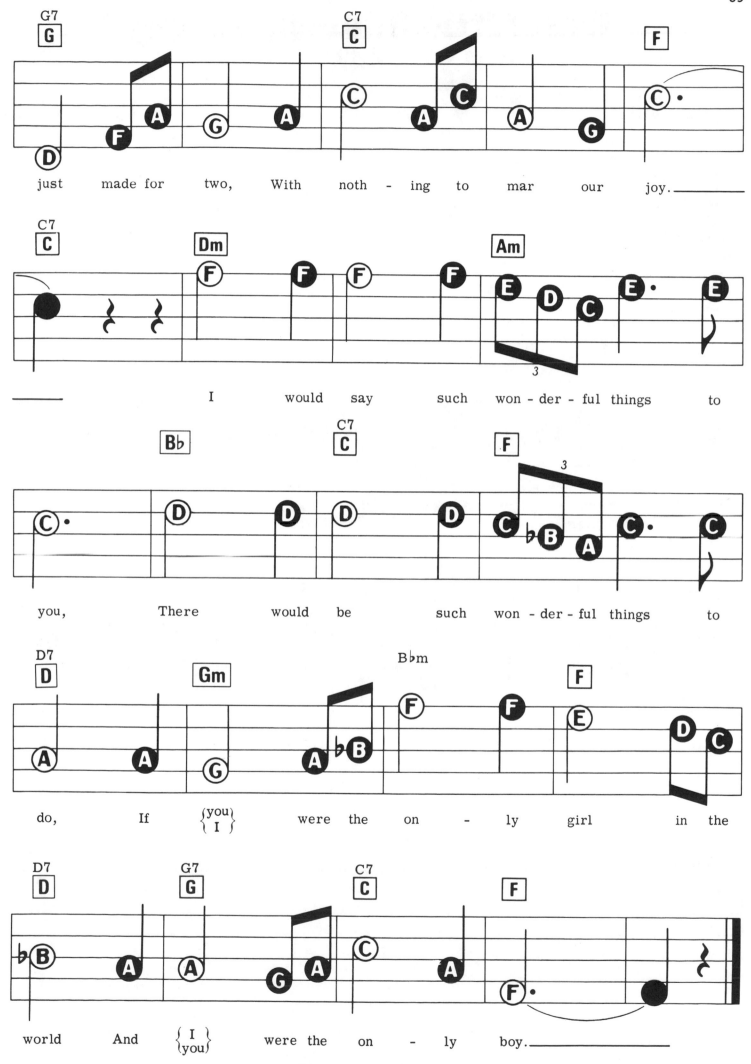

In A Little Spanish Town
('Twas On A Night Like This)

Registration 3
Rhythm: Waltz

Words by Sam M. Lewis and Joe Young
Music by Mabel Wayne

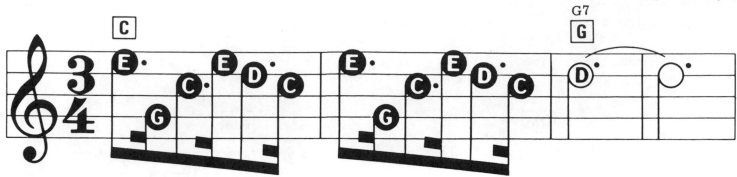

In a lit - tle Span - ish town, 'twas on a night like this,_____

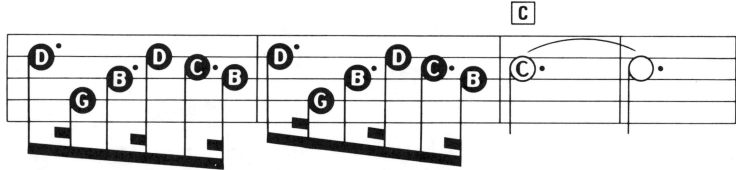

Stars were peek - a - boo - ing down, 'twas on a night like this,_____

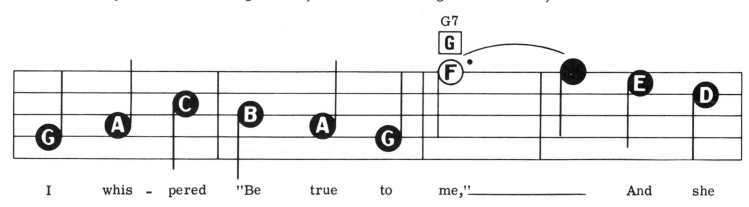

I whis - pered "Be true to me,"_____ And she

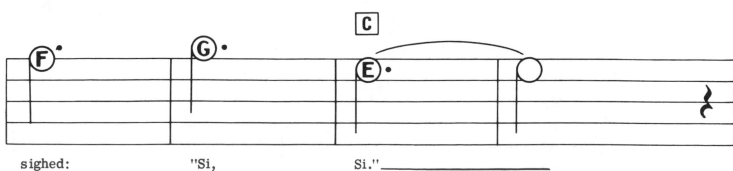

sighed: "Si, Si."_____

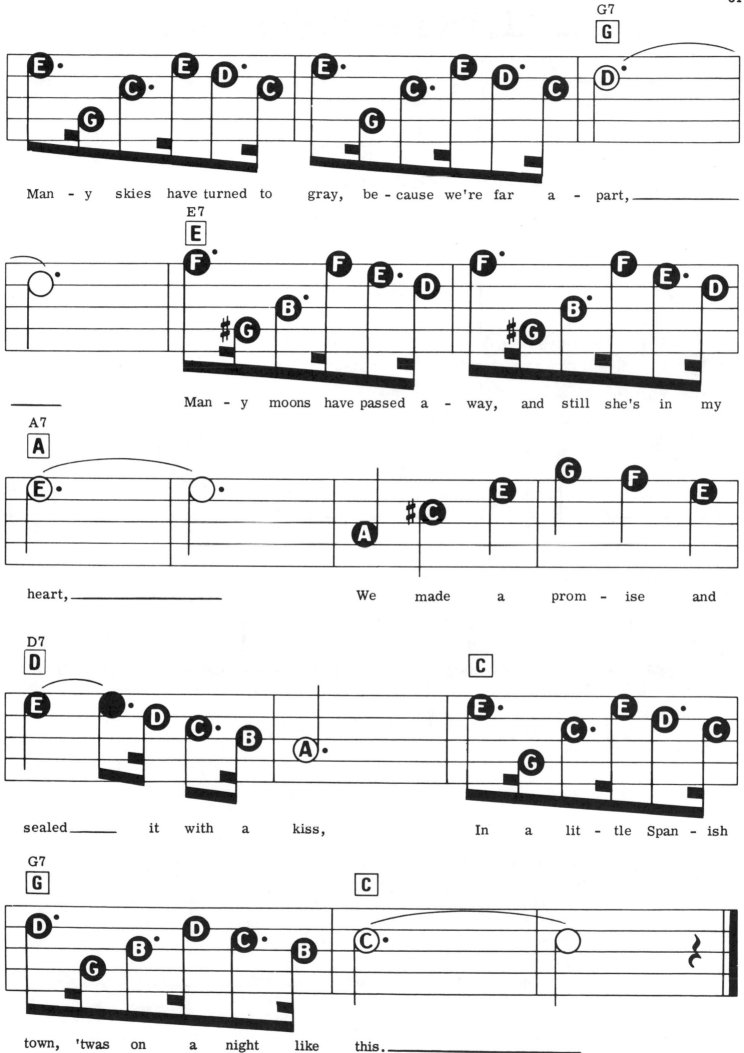

Man - y skies have turned to gray, be - cause we're far a - part,_____

_____ Man - y moons have passed a - way, and still she's in my

heart,_____ We made a prom - ise and

sealed_____ it with a kiss, In a lit - tle Span - ish

town, 'twas on a night like this._____

It All Depends On You

Registration 7
Rhythm: Fox Trot or Swing

Words and Music by B.G. DeSylva,
Lew Brown and Ray Henderson

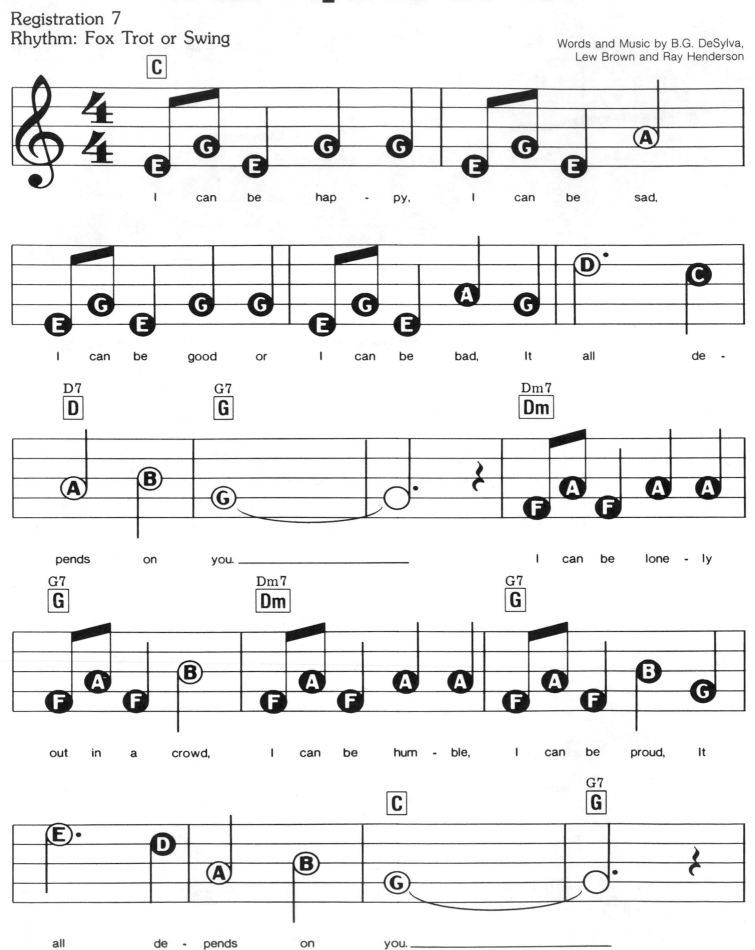

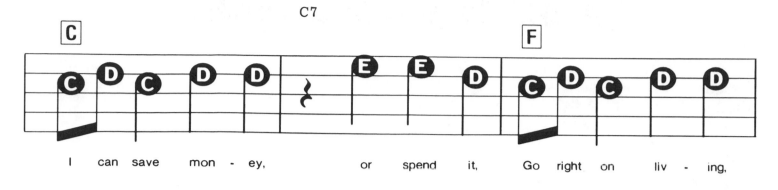

I can save mon - ey, or spend it, Go right on liv - ing,

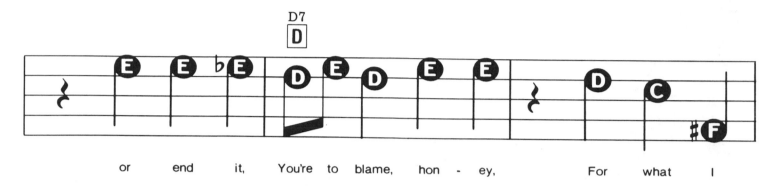

or end it, You're to blame, hon - ey, For what I

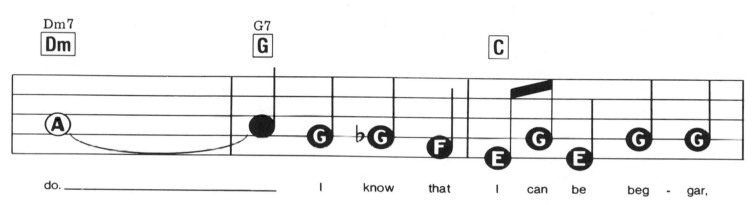

do. _____ I know that I can be beg - gar,

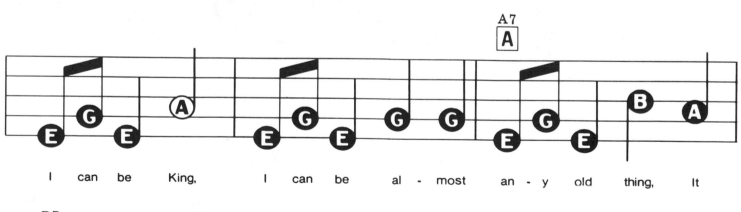

I can be King, I can be al - most an - y old thing, It

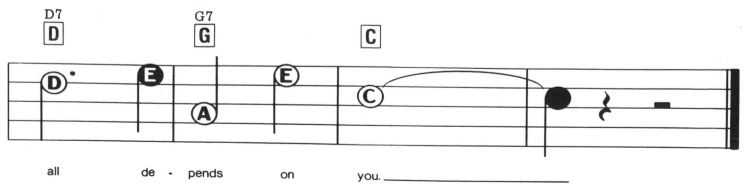

all de - pends on you. _____

Let A Smile Be Your Umbrella

Registration 5
Rhythm: Fox Trot

Words by Irving Kahal & Francis Wheeler
Music by Sammy Fain

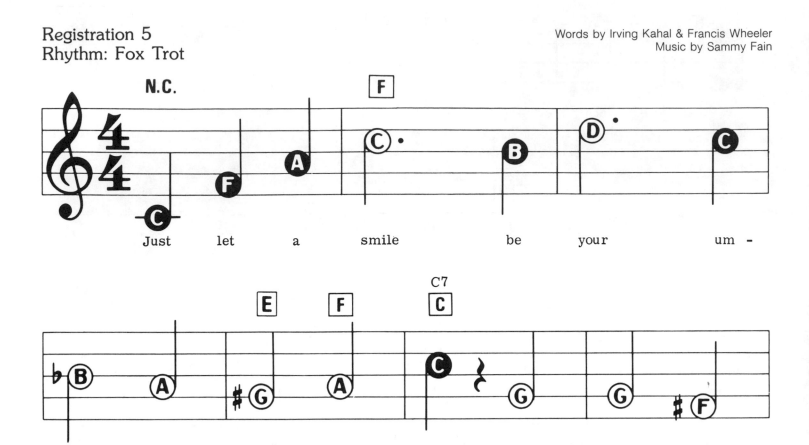

Just let a smile be your um -

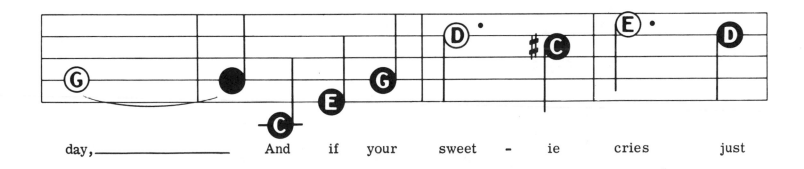

brel - la on a rain - y, rain - y

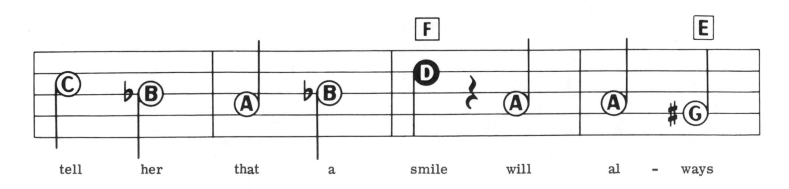

day, _____ And if your sweet - ie cries just

tell her that a smile will al - ways

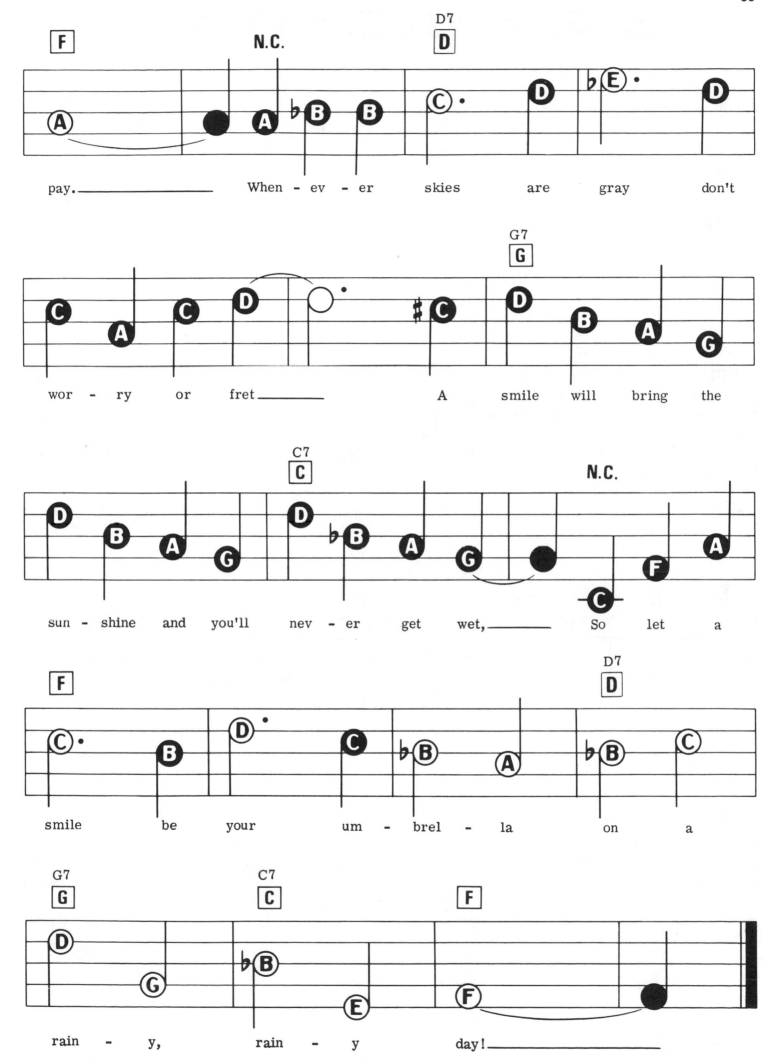

Look For The Silver Lining

Registration 2
Rhythm: Fox Trot or Swing

Words by Buddy DeSylva
Music by Jerome Kern

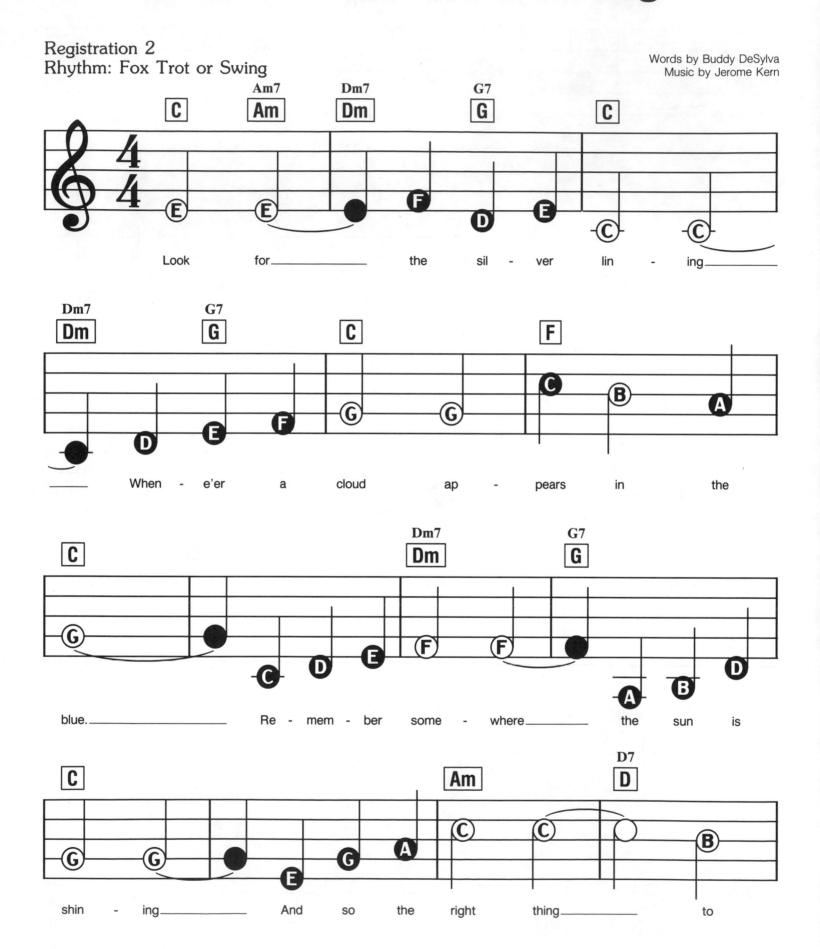

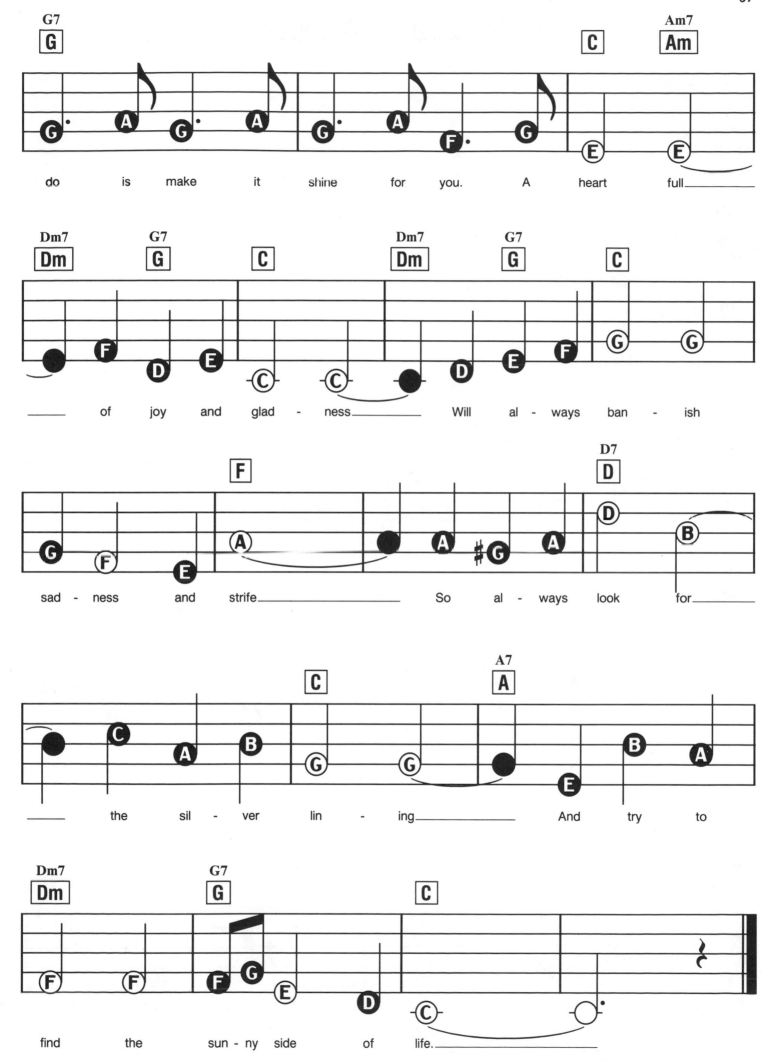

Make Believe

Registration 10
Rhythm: Fox Trot or Swing

Words by Oscar Hammerstein II
Music by Jerome Kern

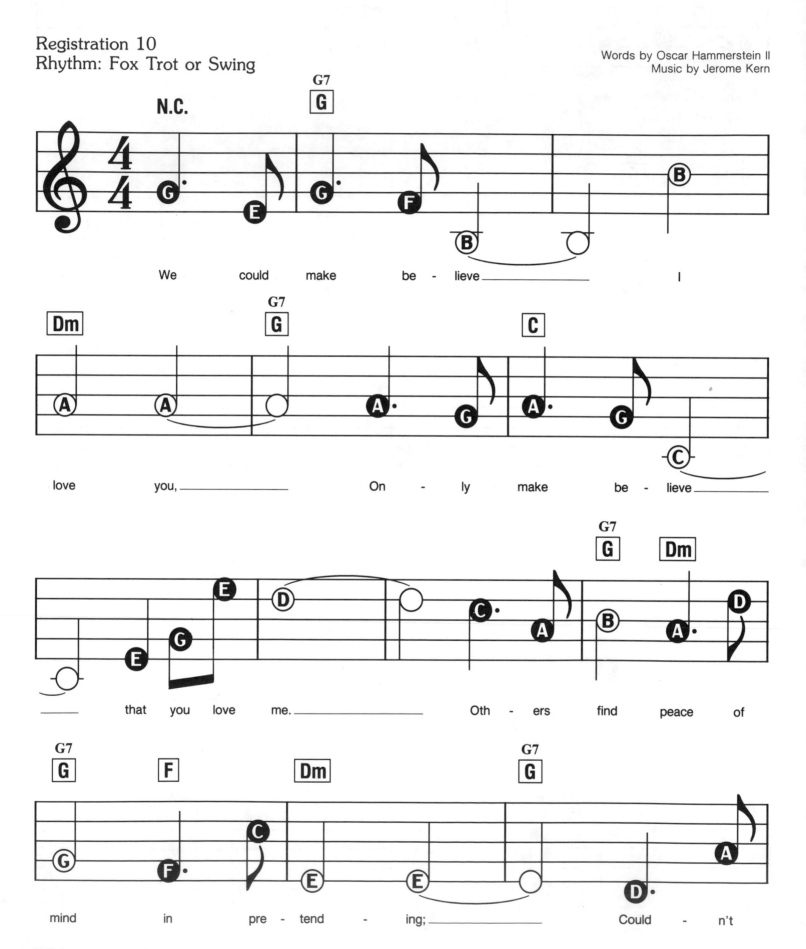

We could make be - lieve _____ I
love you, _____ On - ly make be - lieve _____
_____ that you love me. _____ Oth - ers find peace of
mind in pre - tend - ing; _____ Could - n't

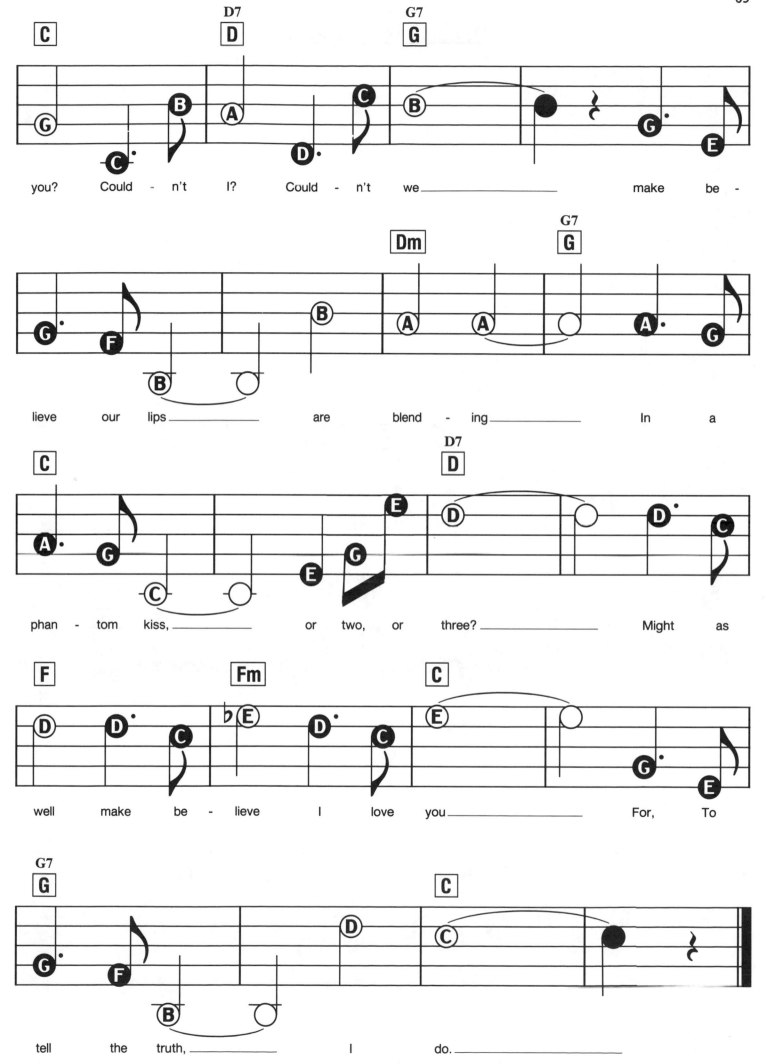

Manhattan

(From the Broadway Musical "GARRICK GAITIES")

Registration 7
Rhythm: Fox Trot

Lyric by Lorenz Hart
Music by Richard Rodgers

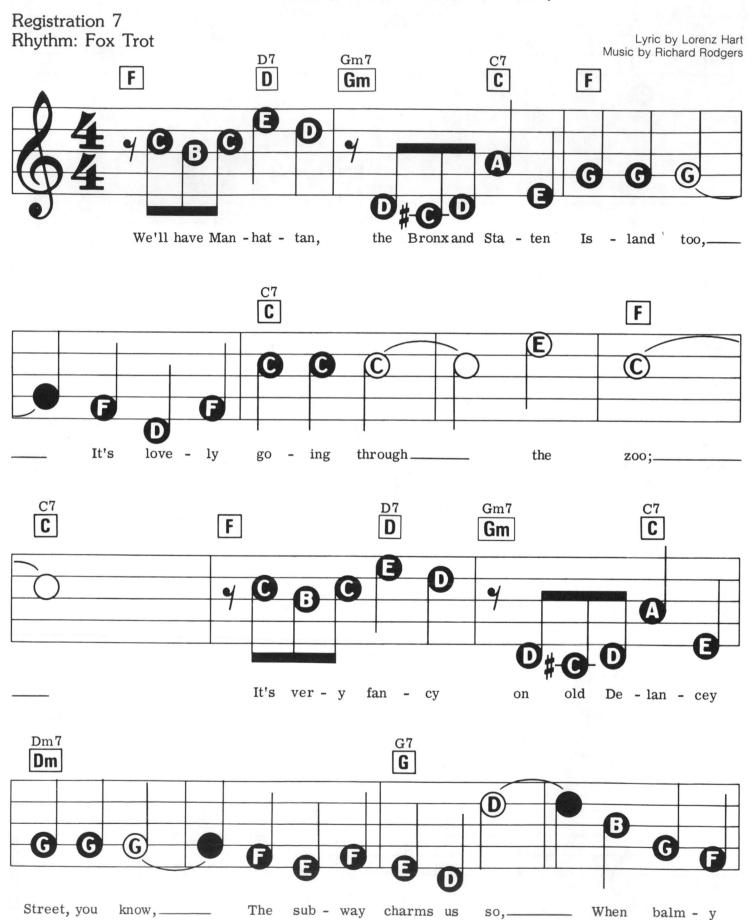

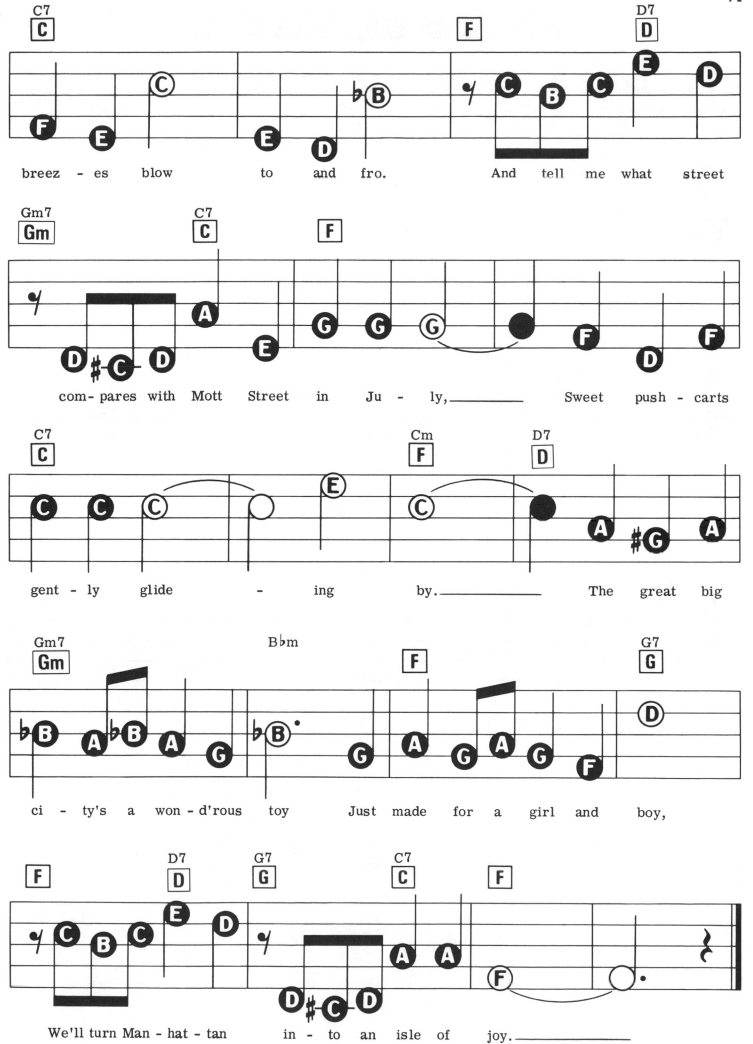

Me And My Shadow

Registration 6
Rhythm: Swing

Words by Billy Rose
Music by Al Jolson and Dave Dreyer

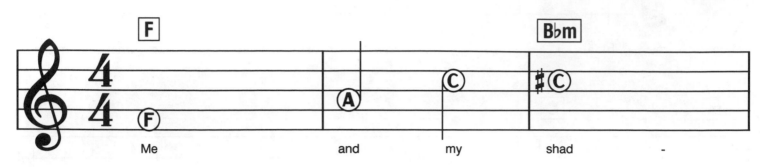

Me   and   my   shad -

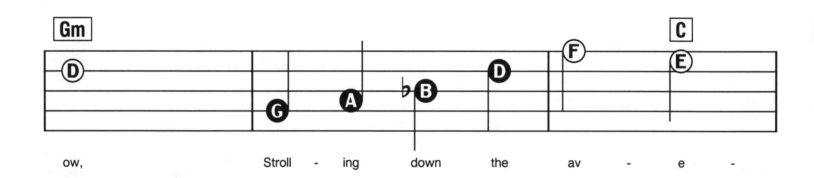

ow,   Stroll - ing   down   the   av - e -

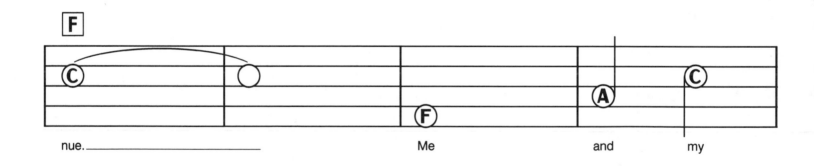

nue._____   Me   and   my

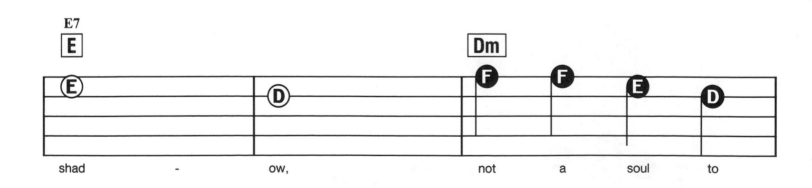

shad - ow,   not   a   soul   to

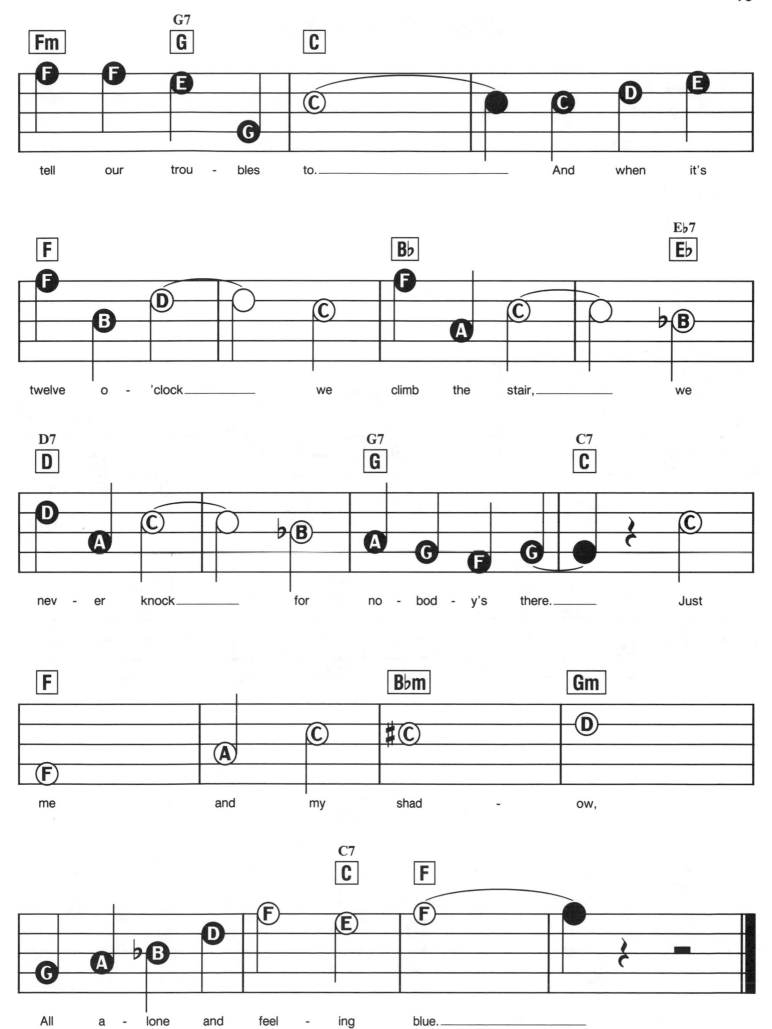

Mean To Me

Registration 4
Rhythm: Swing

Words and Music by
Fred B. Ahlert and Roy Turk

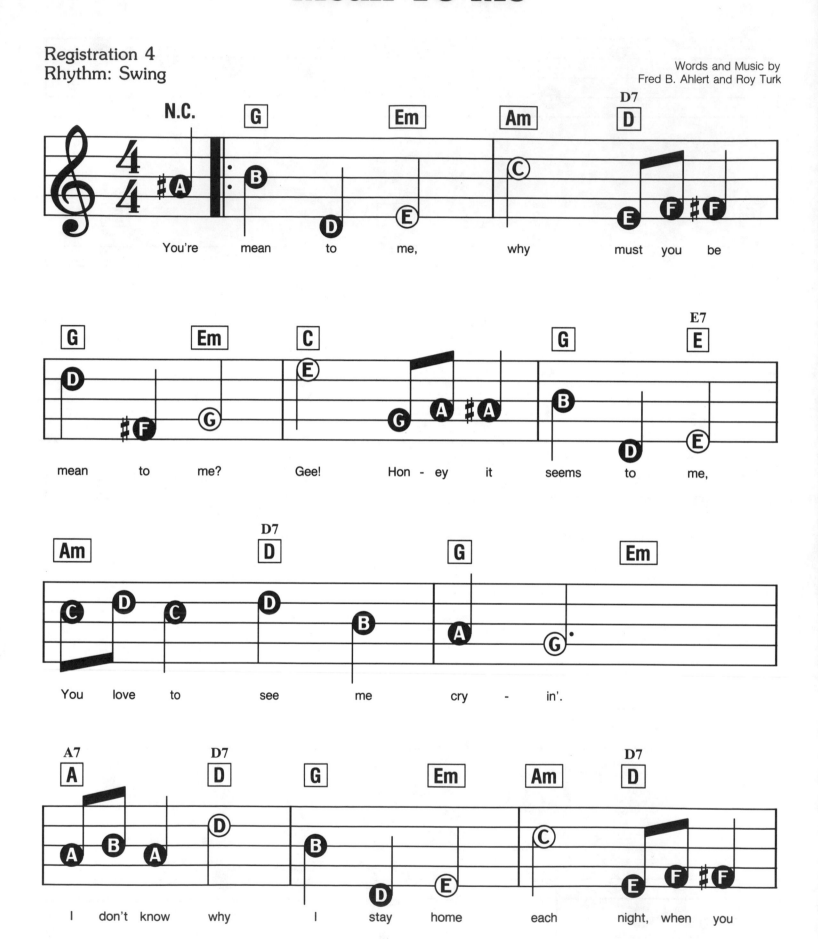

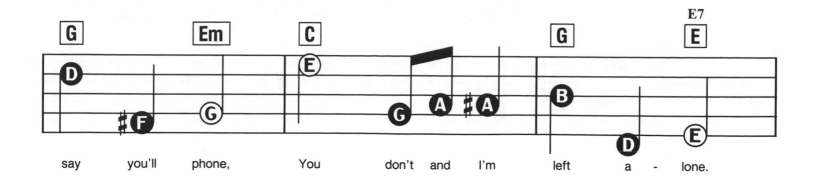

say   you'll   phone,   You   don't   and   I'm   left   a - lone.

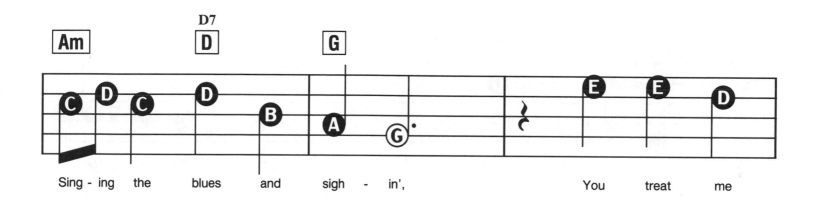

Sing - ing   the   blues   and   sigh - in',   You   treat   me

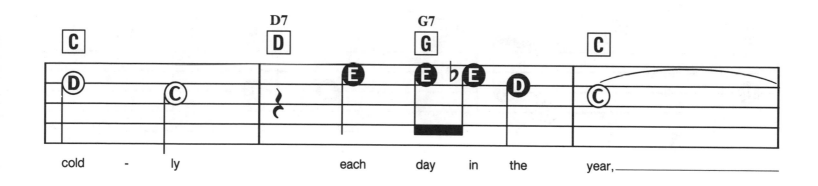

cold - ly   each   day   in   the   year,_____

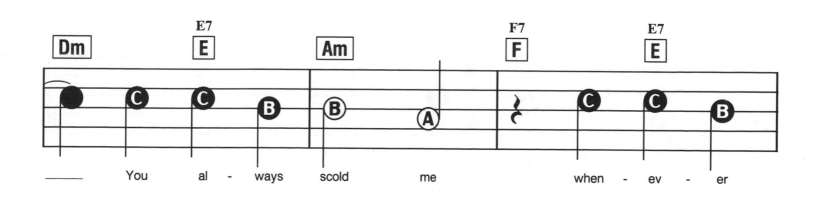

_____   You   al - ways   scold   me   when - ev - er

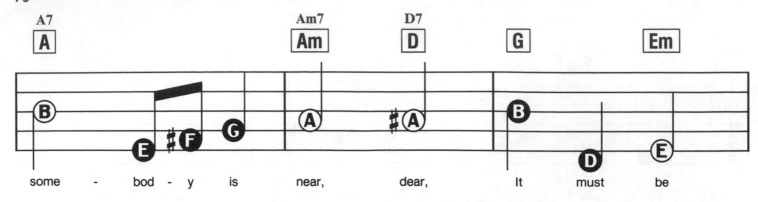

some - bod - y is near, dear, It must be

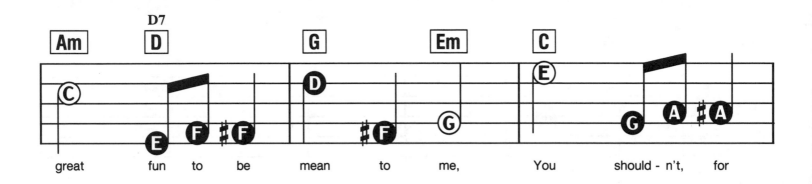

great fun to be mean to me, You should - n't, for

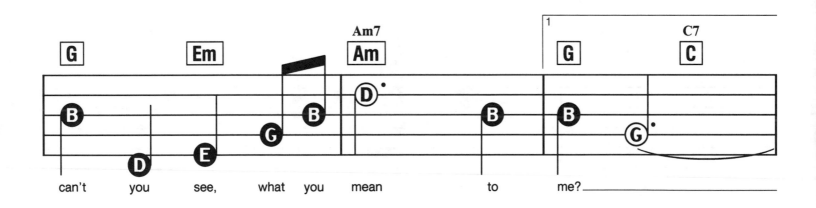

can't you see, what you mean to me?

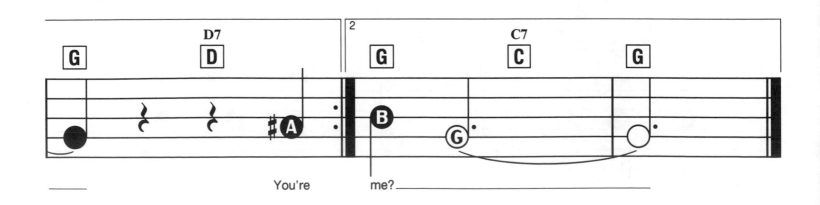

You're me?

Miss You

Registration 1
Rhythm: Swing

Words by Charles Tobias and Harry Tobias
Music by Henry H. Tobias

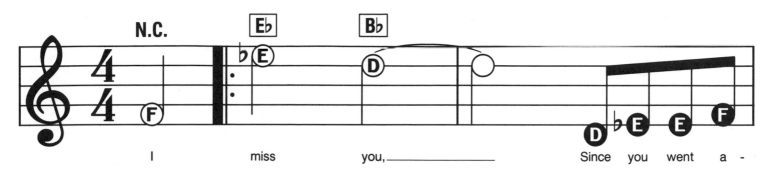

I miss you,_____ Since you went a -

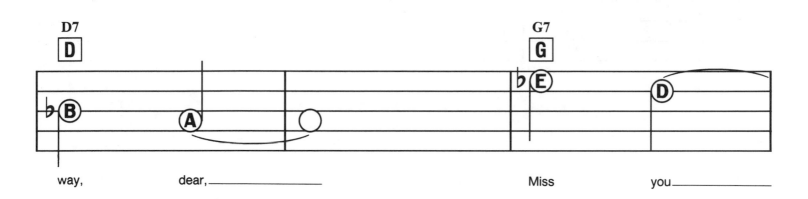

way, dear,_____ Miss you_____

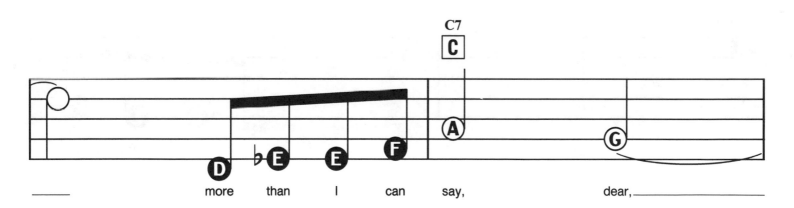

_____ more than I can say, dear,_____

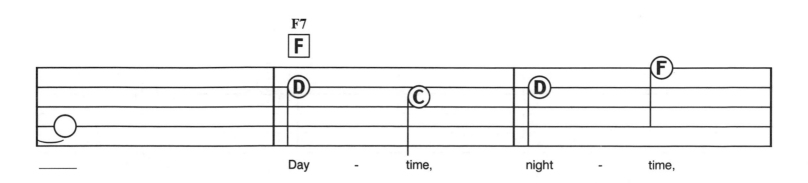

_____ Day - time, night - time,

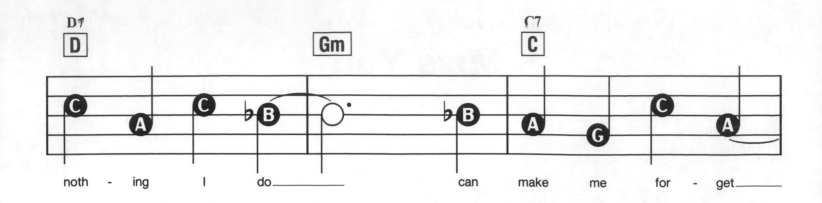

nothing I do_____ can make me for - get_____

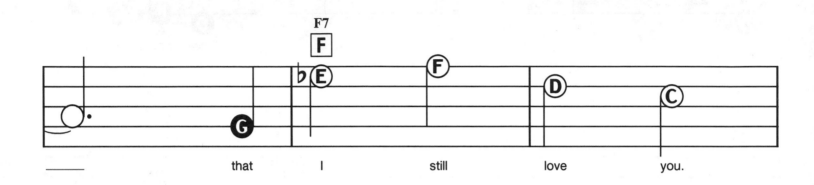

_____ that I still love you.

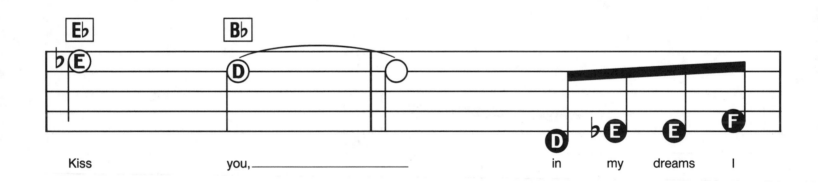

Kiss you,_____ in my dreams I

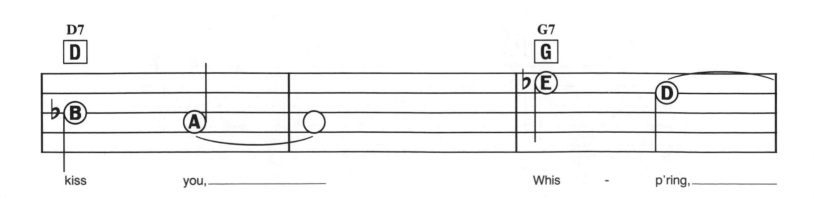

kiss you,_____ Whis - p'ring,_____

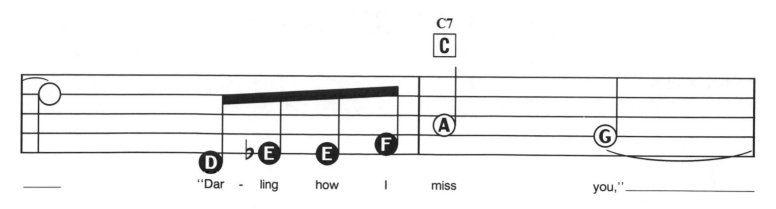

"Dar - ling how I miss you,"

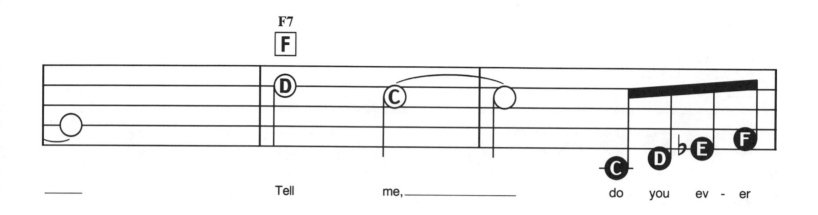

Tell me, do you ev - er

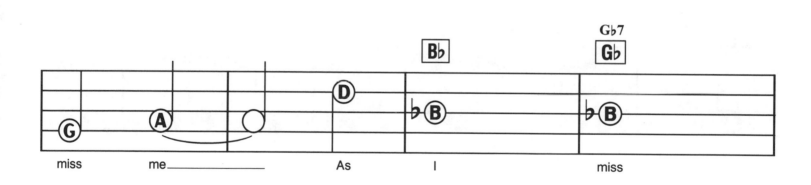

miss me As I miss

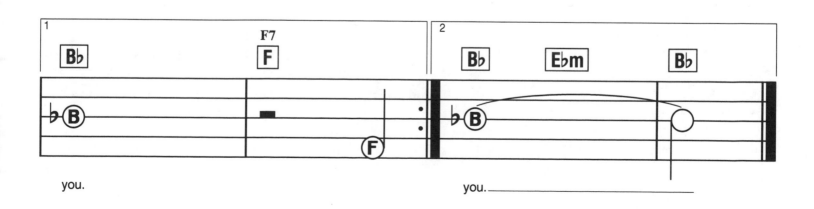

you. you.

Mississippi Mud

Registration 4
Rhythm: Swing

By James Cavanaugh and Harry Barris

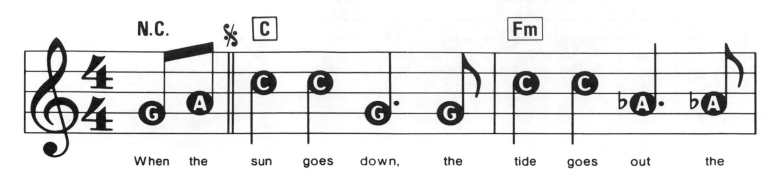

When the sun goes down, the tide goes out the

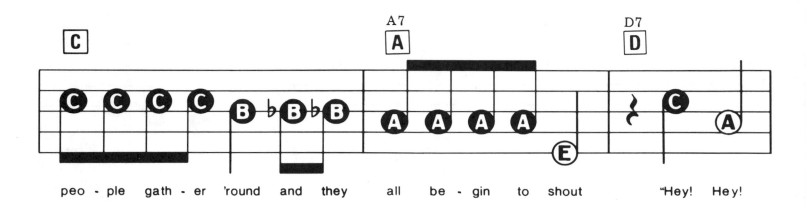

peo - ple gath - er 'round and they all be - gin to shout "Hey! Hey!

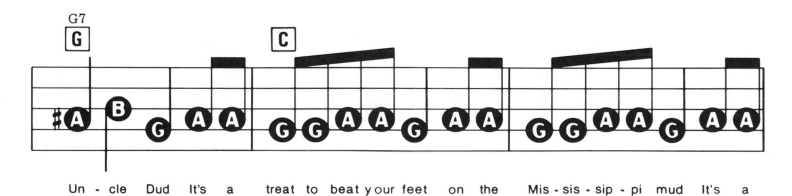

Un - cle Dud It's a treat to beat your feet on the Mis - sis - sip - pi mud It's a

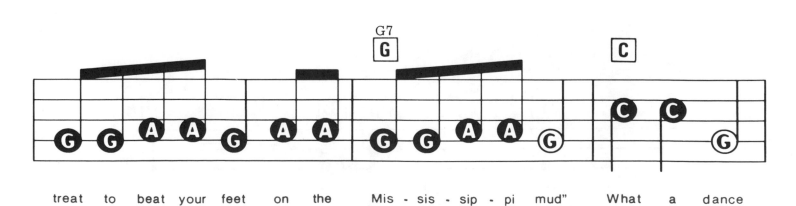

treat to beat your feet on the Mis - sis - sip - pi mud" What a dance

81

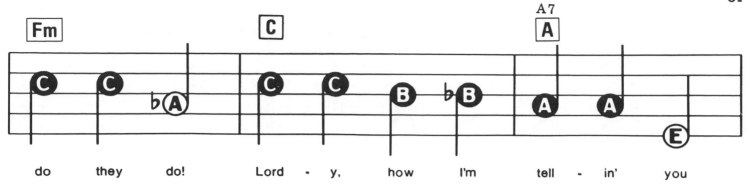

do they do! Lord - y, how I'm tell - in' you

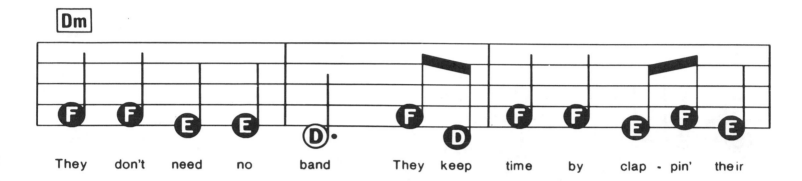

They don't need no band They keep time by clap - pin' their

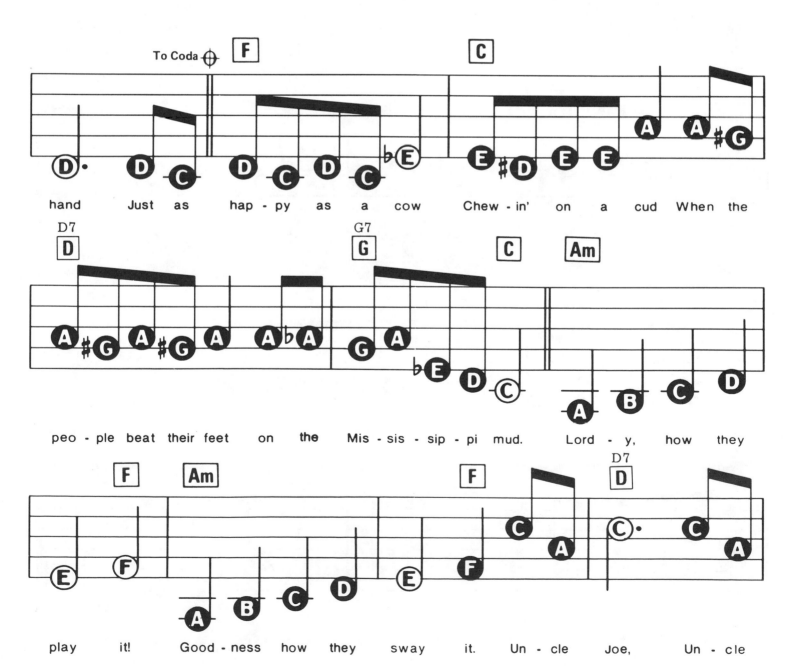

hand Just as hap - py as a cow Chew - in' on a cud When the

peo - ple beat their feet on the Mis - sis - sip - pi mud. Lord - y, how they

play it! Good - ness how they sway it. Un - cle Joe, Un - cle

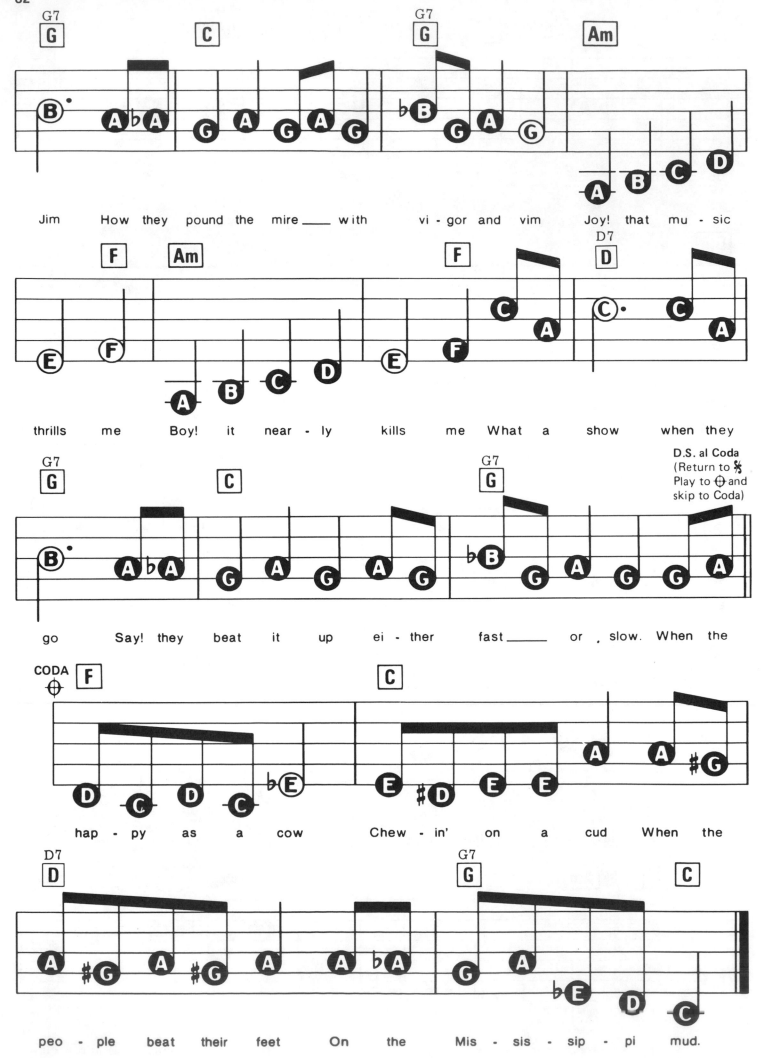

More Than You Know

Registration 8
Rhythm: Fox Trot

Words by William Rose and Edward Eliscu
Music by Vincent Youmans

84

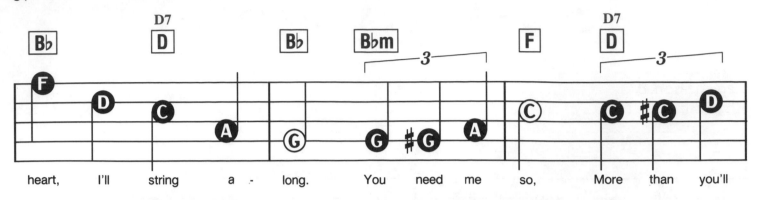

heart, I'll string a - long. You need me so, More than you'll

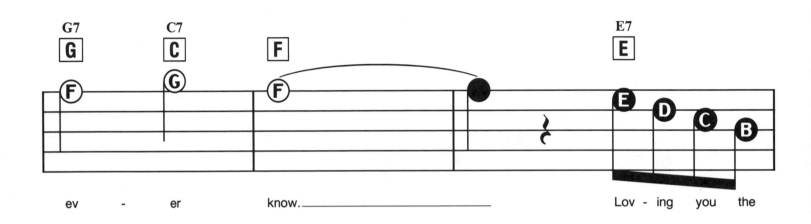

ev - er know. Lov - ing you the

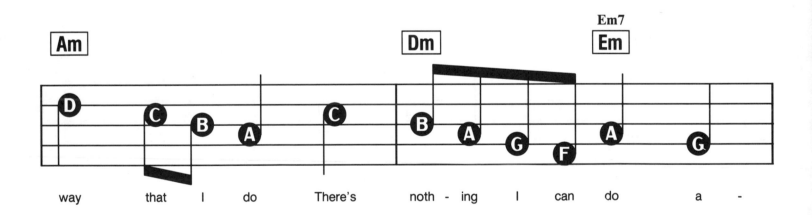

way that I do There's noth - ing I can do a -

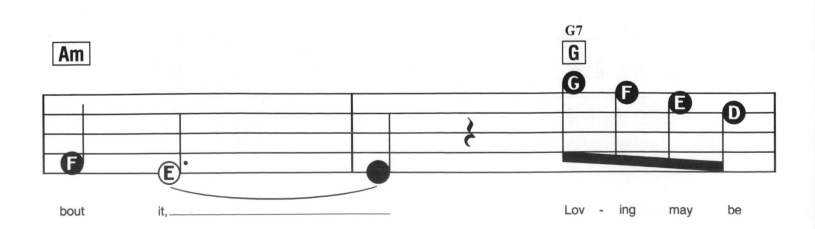

bout it, Lov - ing may be

85

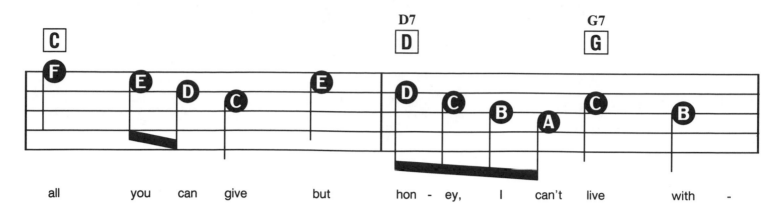

all you can give but hon - ey, I can't live with -

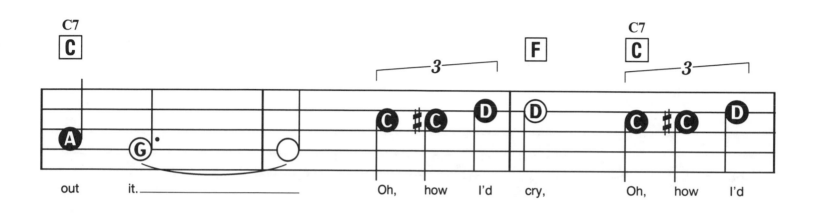

out it. Oh, how I'd cry, Oh, how I'd

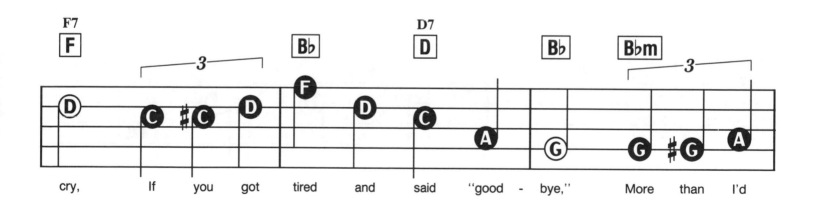

cry, If you got tired and said "good - bye," More than I'd

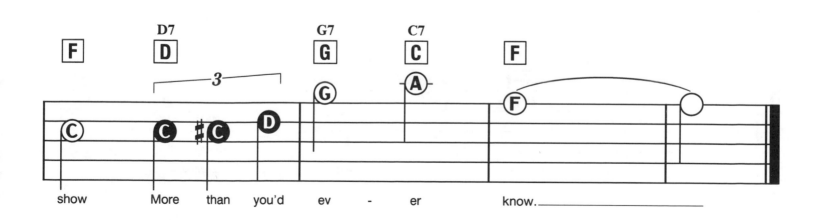

show More than you'd ev - er know.

Moonlight And Roses
(Bring Mem'ries Of You)

Registration 9
Rhythm: Ballad or Fox Trot

Words and Music by
Ben Black & Neil Moret

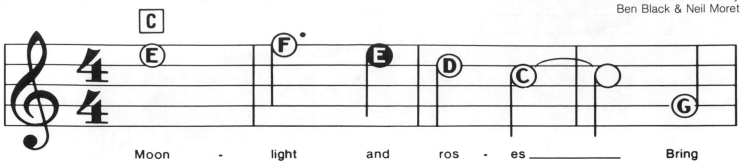

Moon - light and ros - es _____ Bring

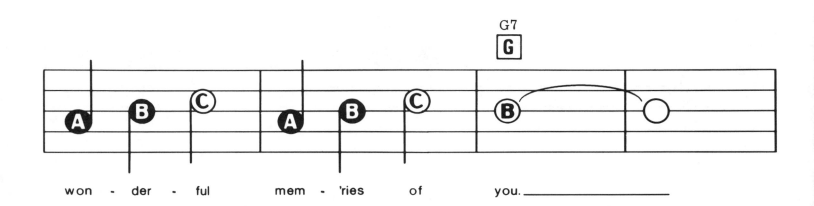

won - der - ful mem - 'ries of you. _____

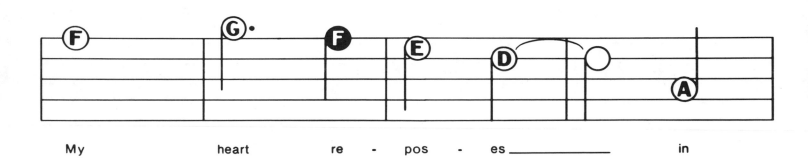

My heart re - pos - es _____ in

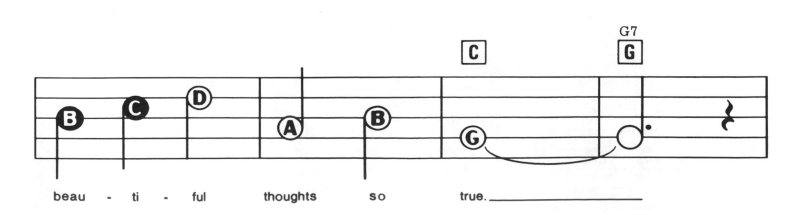

beau - ti - ful thoughts so true. _____

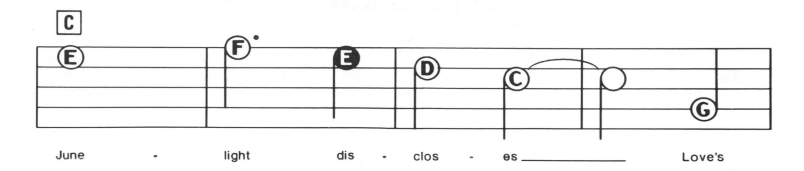

June - light dis - clos - es _____ Love's

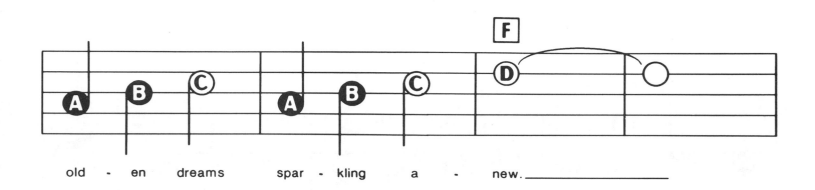

old - en dreams spar - kling a - new. _____

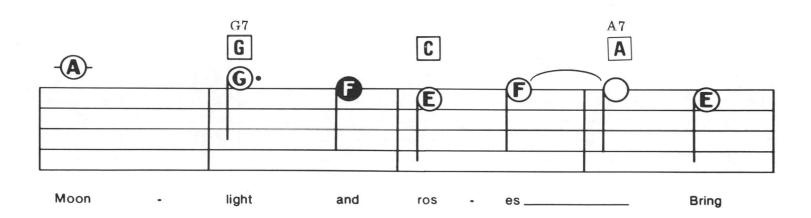

Moon - light and ros - es _____ Bring

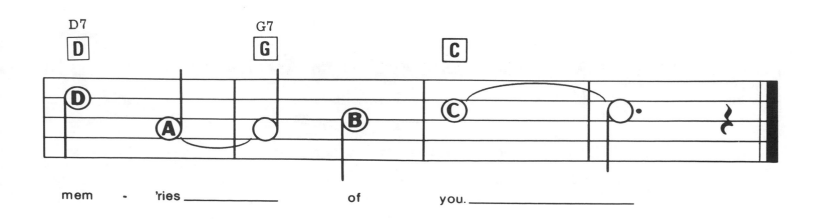

mem - 'ries _____ of you. _____

My Mammy

(From "THE JAZZ SINGER")

Registration 3
Rhythm: Ballad

Words by Sam M. Lewis and Joe Young
Music by Walter Donaldson

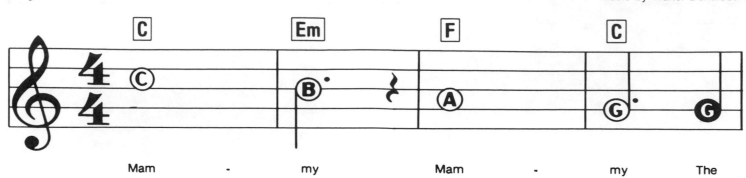

Mam - my Mam - my The

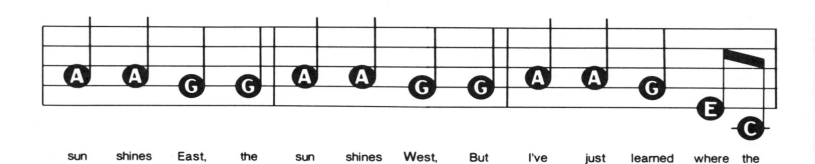

sun shines East, the sun shines West, But I've just learned where the

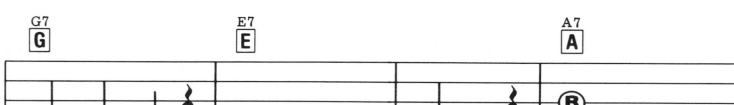

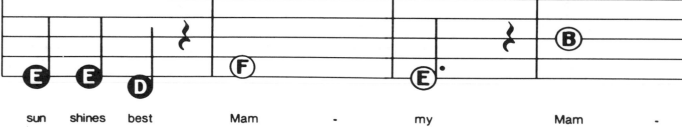

sun shines best Mam - my Mam -

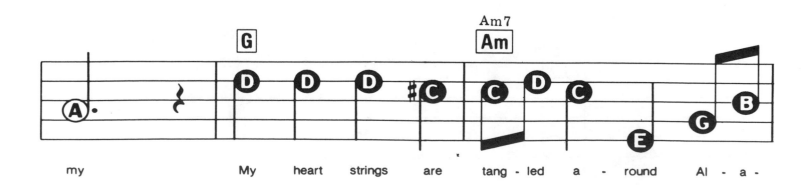

my My heart strings are tang - led a - round Al - a -

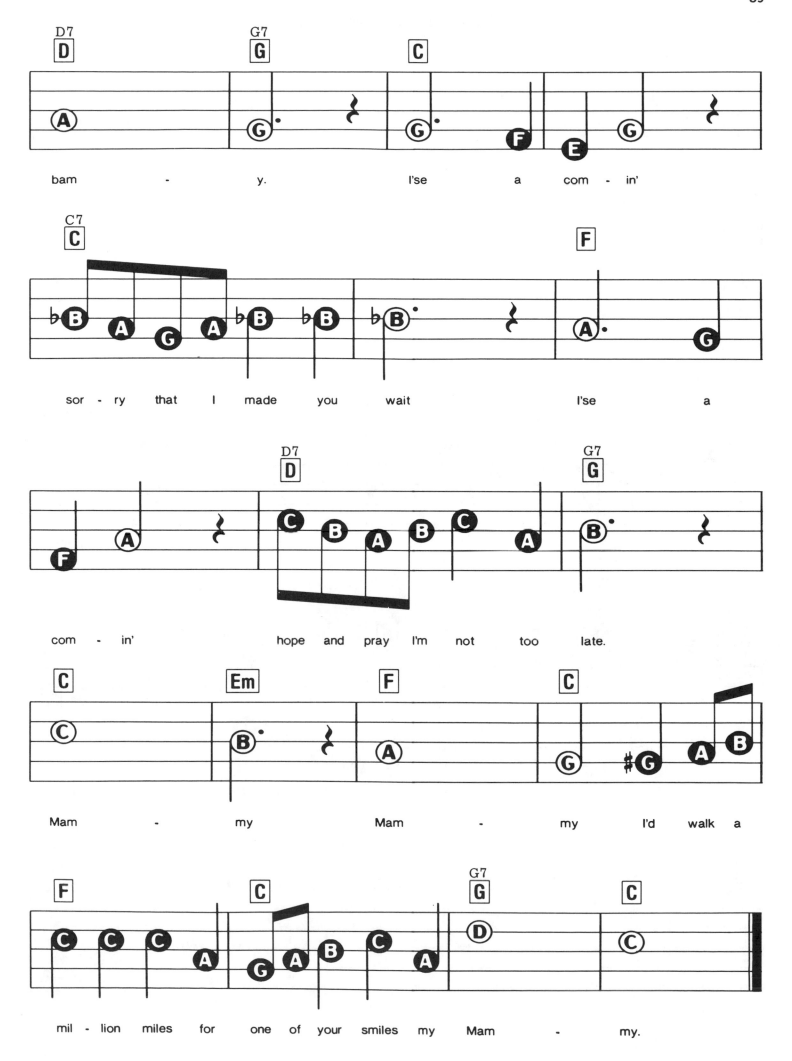

Ol' Man River

Registration 5
Rhythm: Ballad or Fox Trot

Words by Oscar Hammerstein II
Music by Jerome Kern

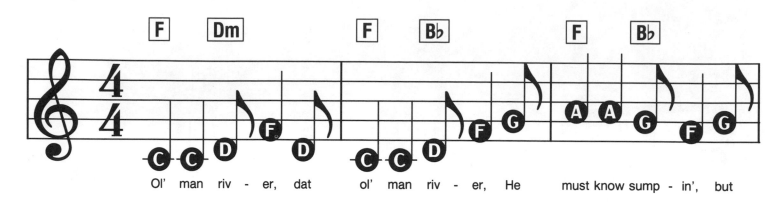

Ol' man riv-er, dat ol' man riv-er, He must know sump-in', but

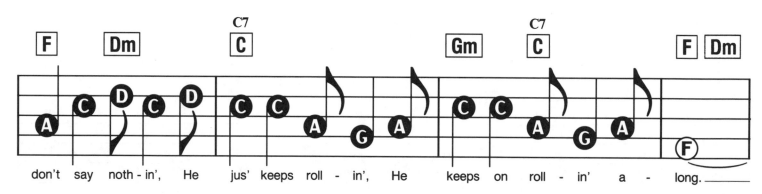

don't say noth-in', He jus' keeps roll-in', He keeps on roll-in' a-long.

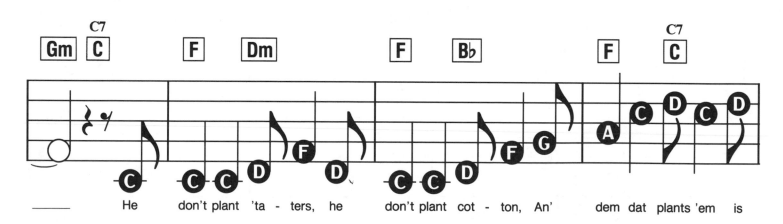

He don't plant 'ta-ters, he don't plant cot-ton, An' dem dat plants 'em is

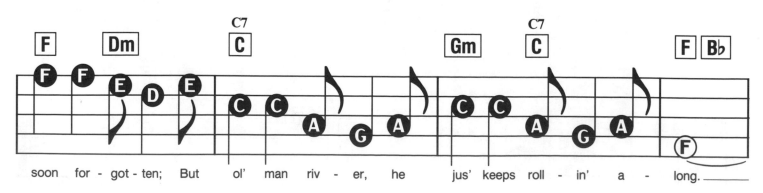

soon for-got-ten; But ol' man riv-er, he jus' keeps roll-in' a-long.

Paddlin' Madelin' Home

Registration 8
Rhythm: Fox Trot or Swing

Words and Music by
Harry Woods

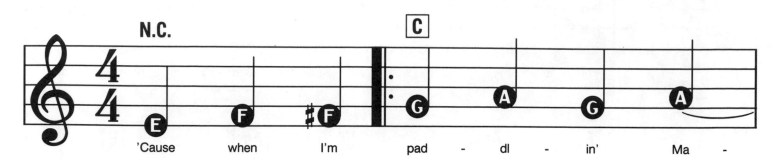

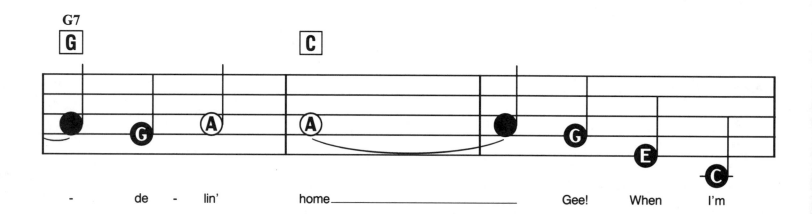

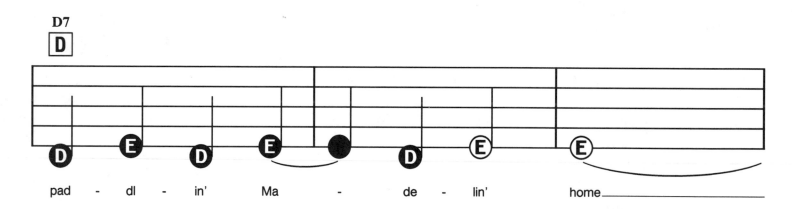

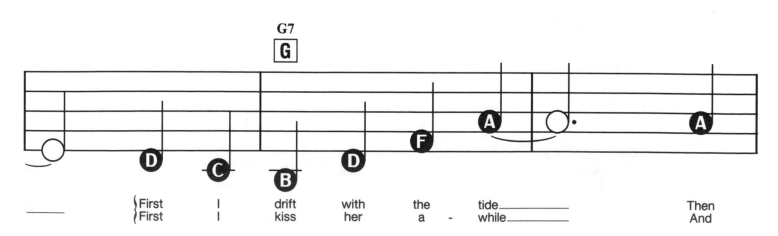

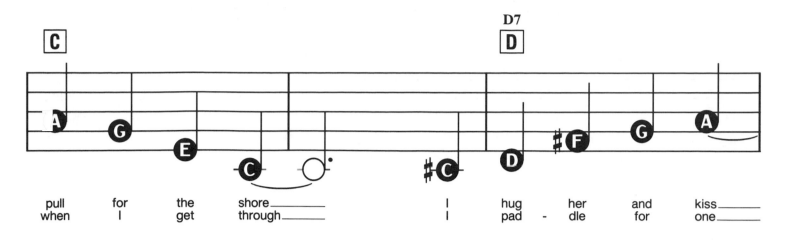

pull for the shore_____ I hug her and kiss_____
when I get through_____ I pad - dle for one_____

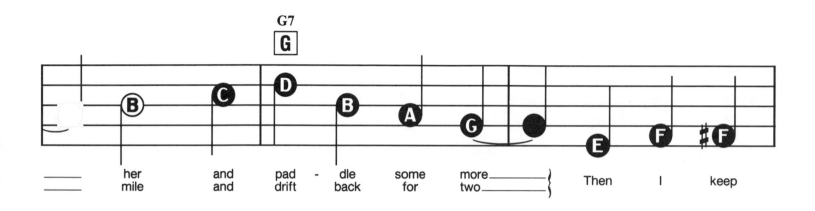

_____ her mile and and pad drift - dle back some for more_____ } Then I keep
two_____

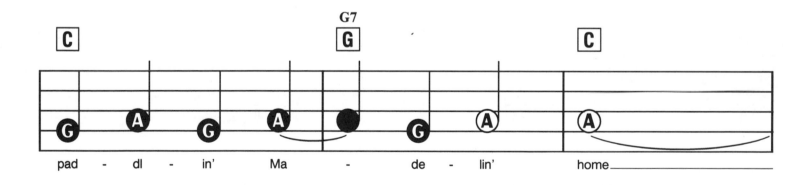

pad - dl - in' Ma - de - lin' home_____

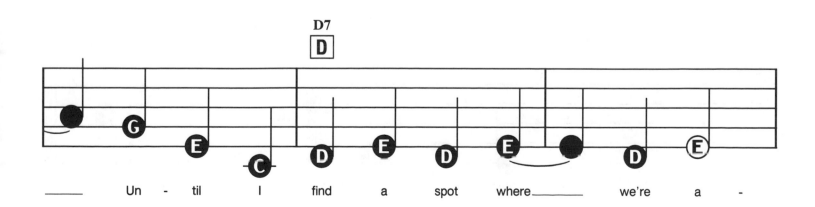

_____ Un - til I find a spot where_____ we're a -

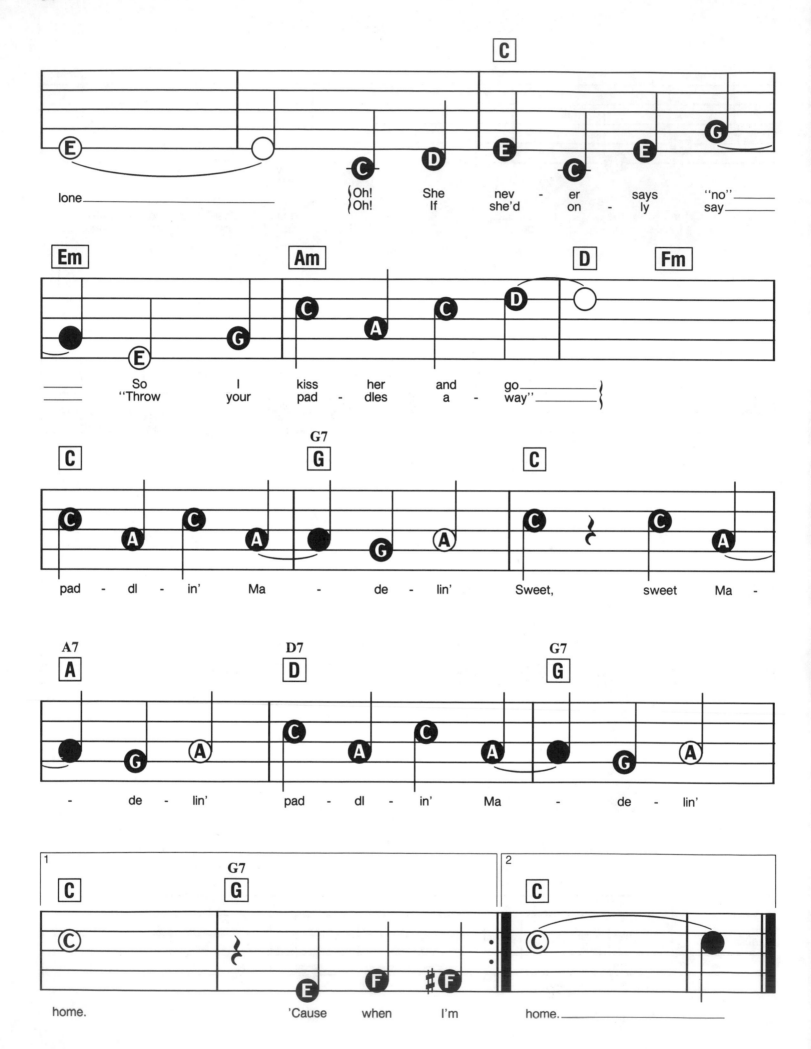

Second Hand Rose

Registration 8
Rhythm: Fox Trot or Swing

Words by Grant Clarke
Music by James F. Hanley

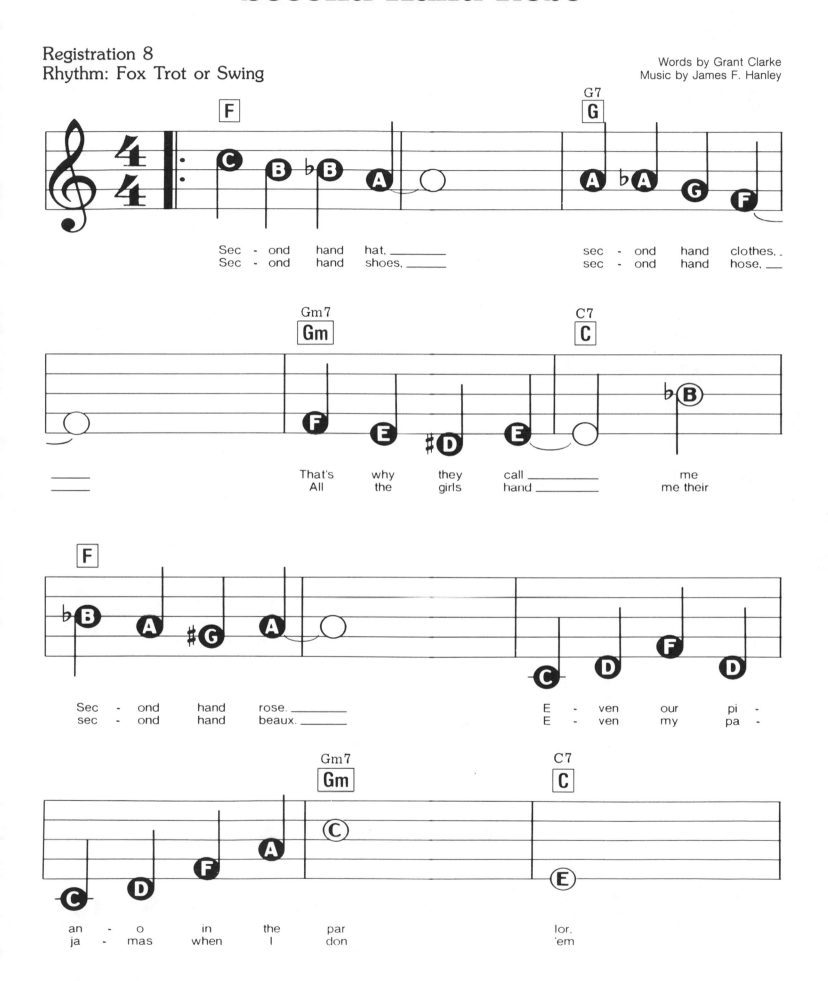

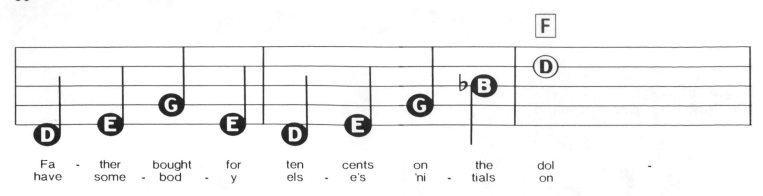

Fa - ther bought for ten cents on the dol -
have some - bod - y els - e's 'ni - tials on

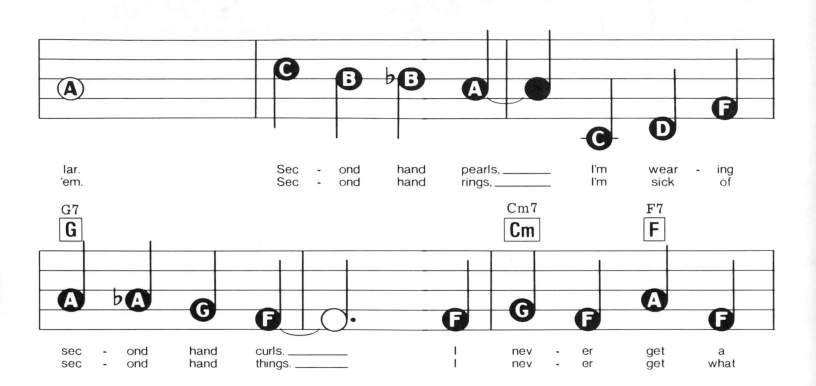

lar.
'em.

Sec - ond hand pearls, _____ I'm wear - ing
Sec - ond hand rings, _____ I'm sick of

G7

Cm7

F7

sec - ond hand curls. _____ I nev - er get a
sec - ond hand things. _____ I nev - er get what

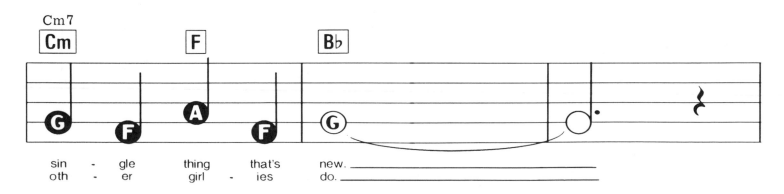

Cm7

sin - gle thing that's new. _____
oth - er girl - ies do. _____

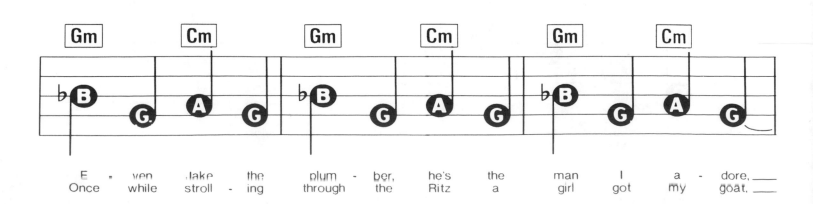

E - ven Jake the plum - ber, he's the man I a - dore, ____
Once while stroll - ing through the Ritz a girl got my goat, ____

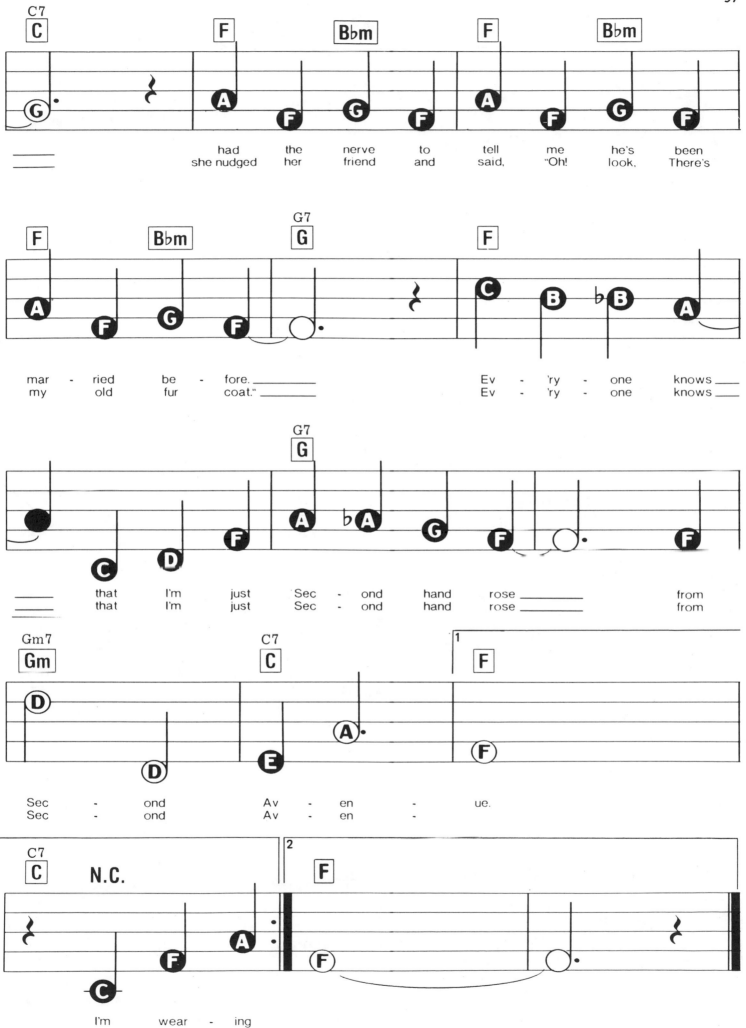

Sentimental Me

Registration 9
Rhythm: Fox Trot

Words by Jimmy Cassin
Music by Jim Morehead

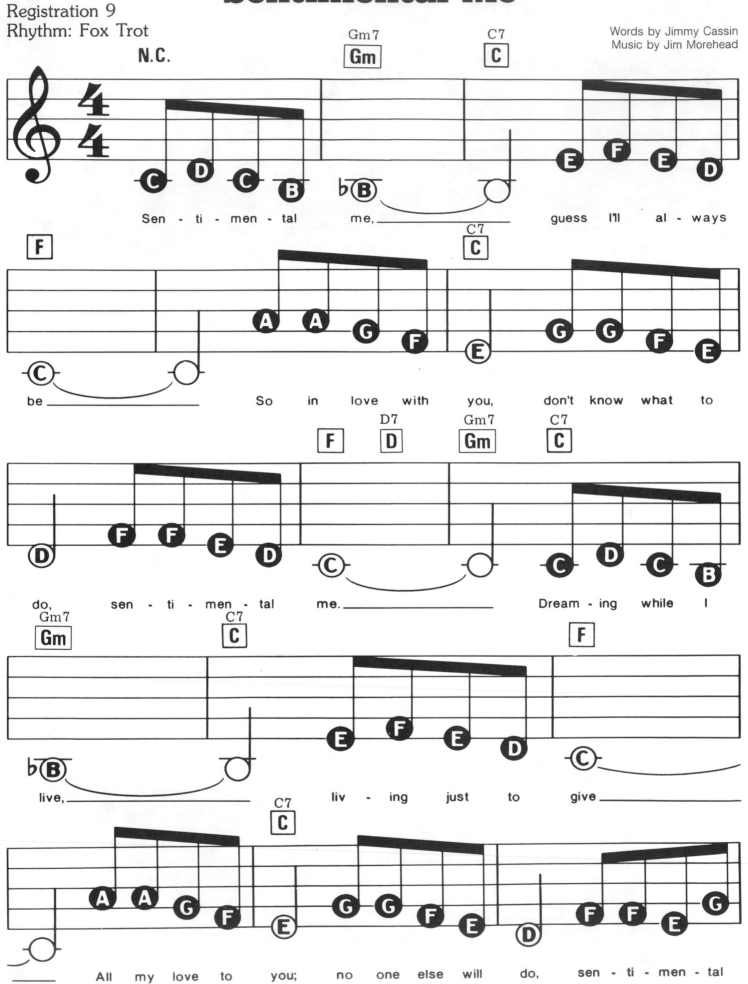

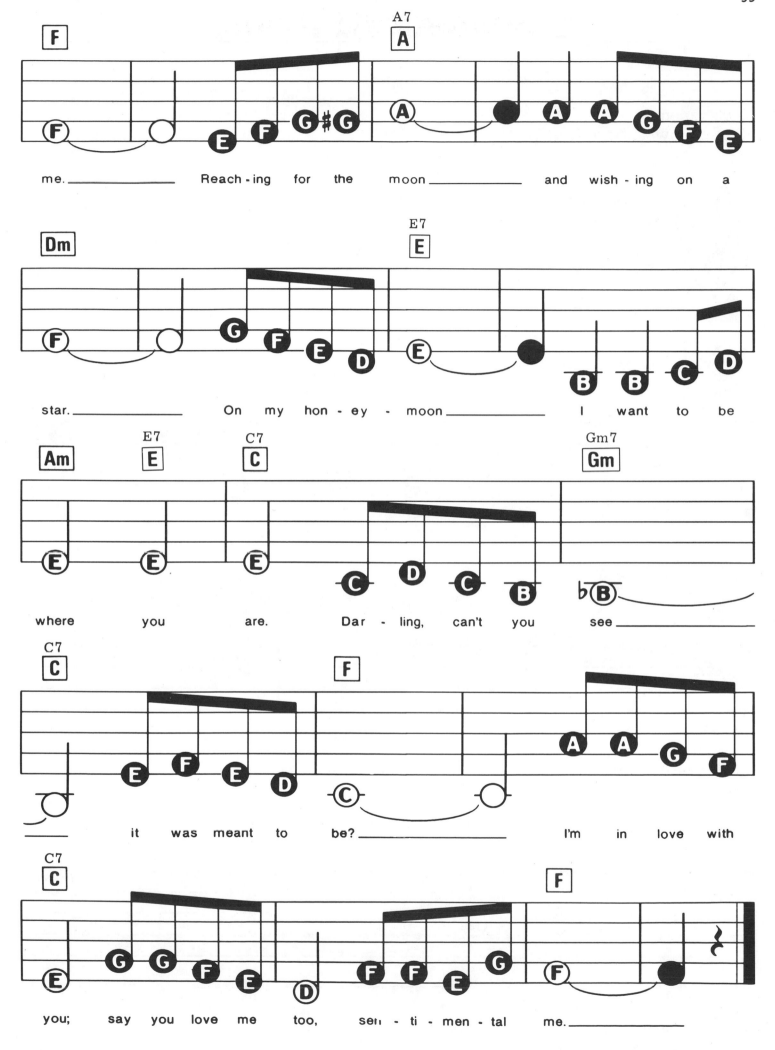

The Sheik Of Araby

Registration 9
Rhythm: Swing or Jazz

Words by Harry B. Smith and Francis Wheeler
Music by Ted Snyder

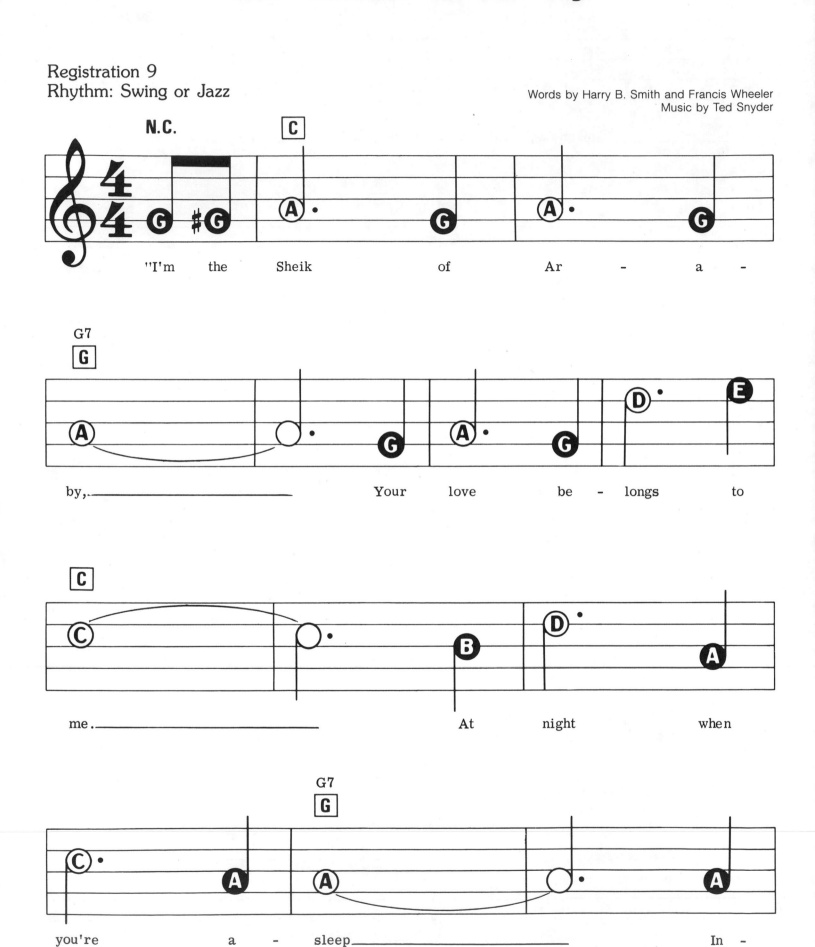

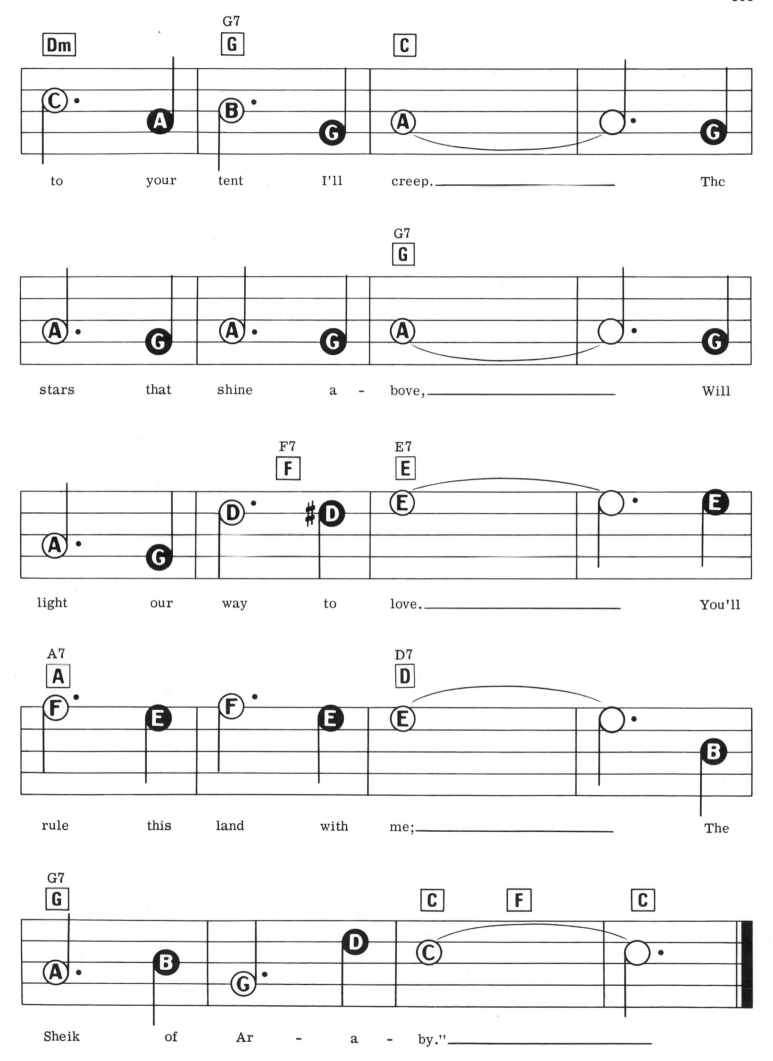

Side By Side

Registration 7
Rhythm: Fox Trot or Swing

Words and Music by
Harry Woods

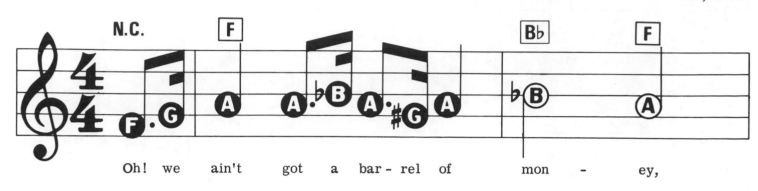

Oh! we ain't got a bar- rel of mon - ey,

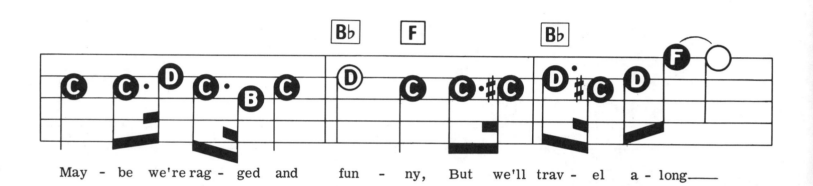

May - be we're rag - ged and fun - ny, But we'll trav - el a - long

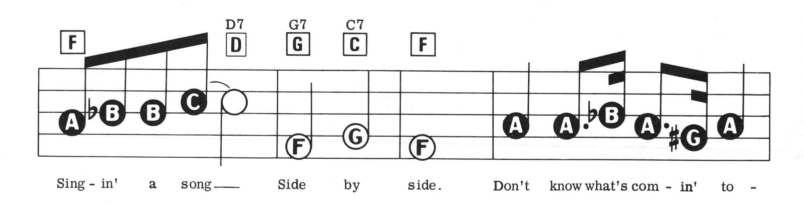

Sing - in' a song Side by side. Don't know what's com - in' to -

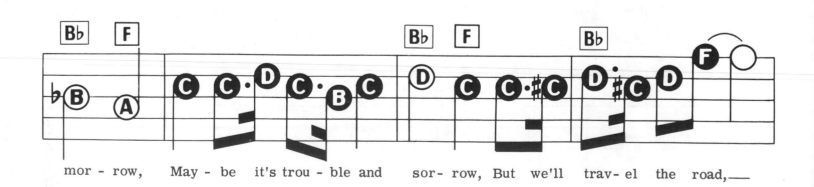

mor - row, May - be it's trou - ble and sor - row, But we'll trav - el the road,

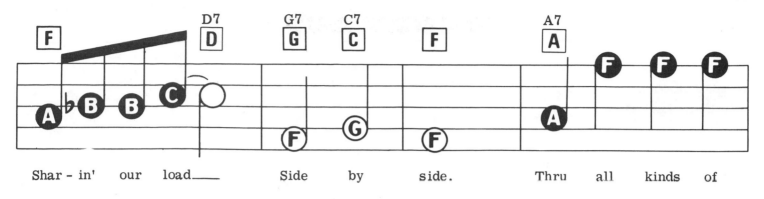

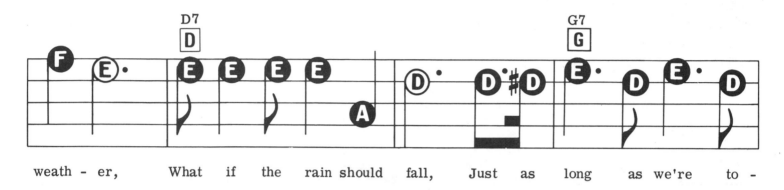

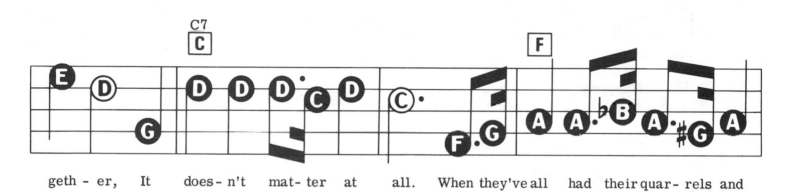

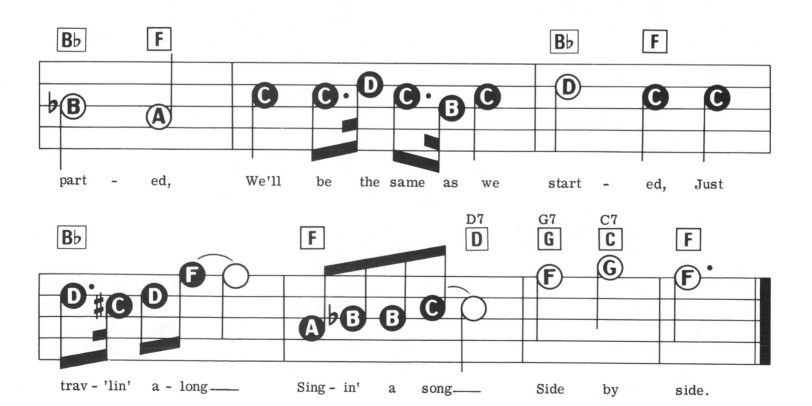

Sonny Boy

Registration 2
Rhythm: Swing

Words and Music by Al Jolson, B.G. DeSylva,
Lew Brown and Ray Henderson

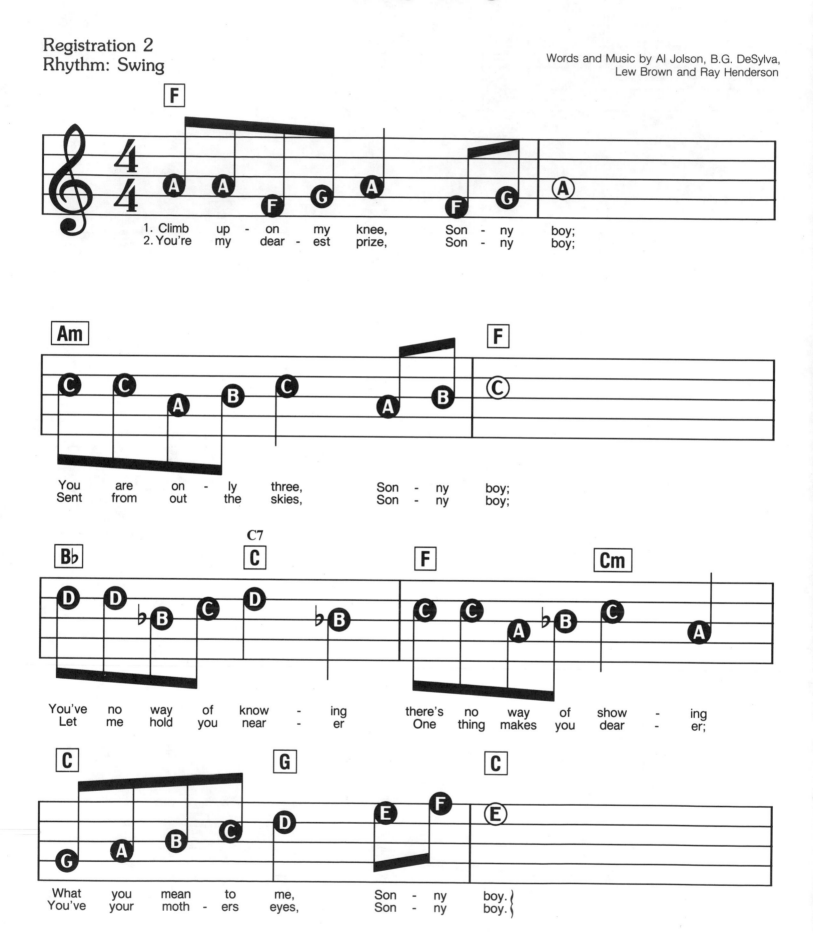

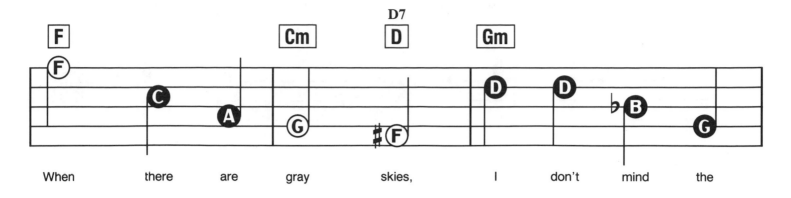

When there are gray skies, I don't mind the

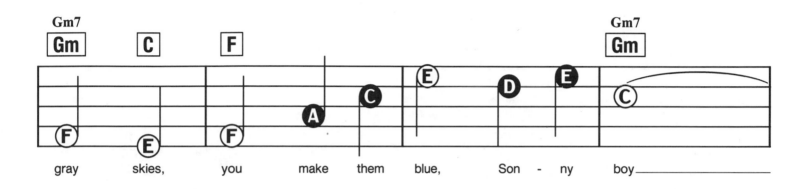

gray skies, you make them blue, Son - ny boy_____

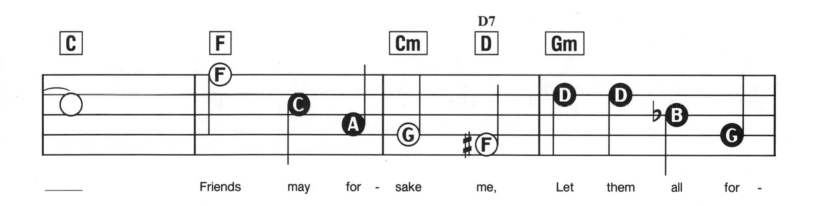

_____ Friends may for - sake me, Let them all for -

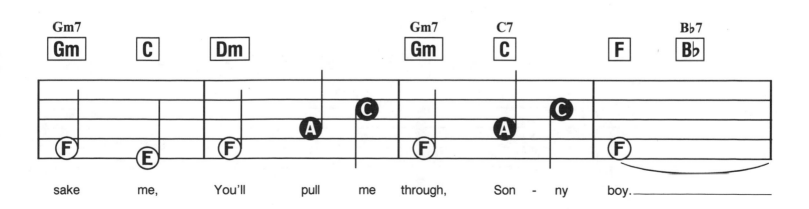

sake me, You'll pull me through, Son - ny boy._____

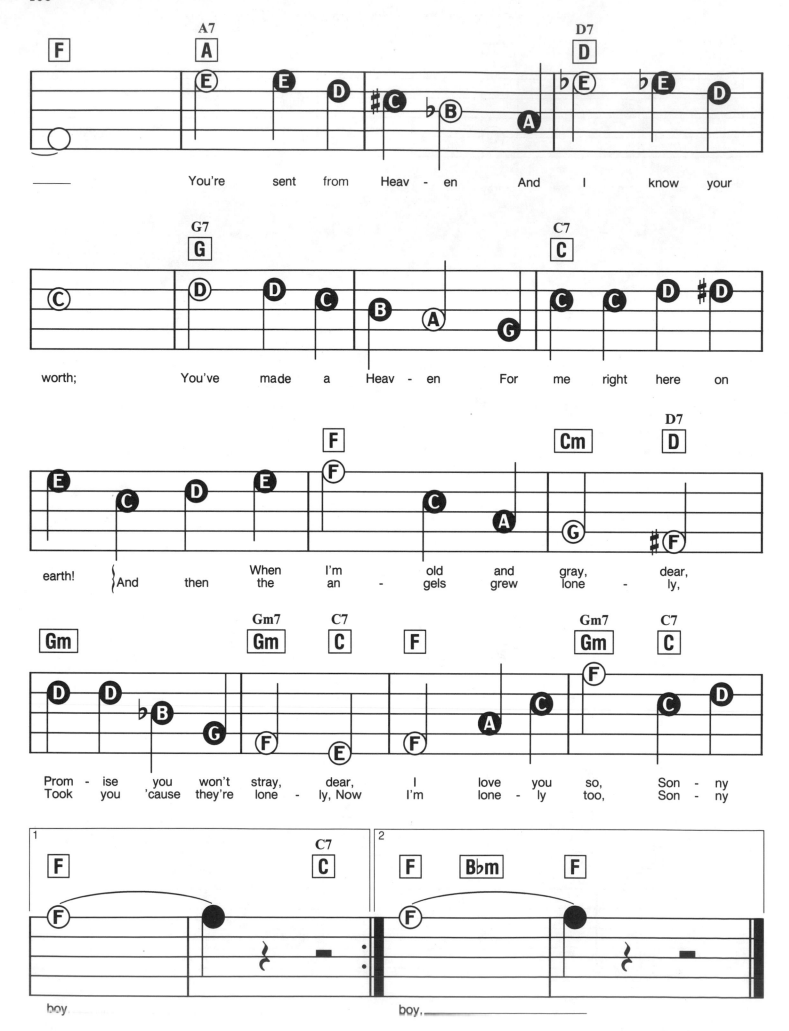

The Wang Wang Blues

Registration 8
Rhythm: Swing

Words and Music by Leo Wood, Gus Mueller,
Buster Johnson and Henry Busse

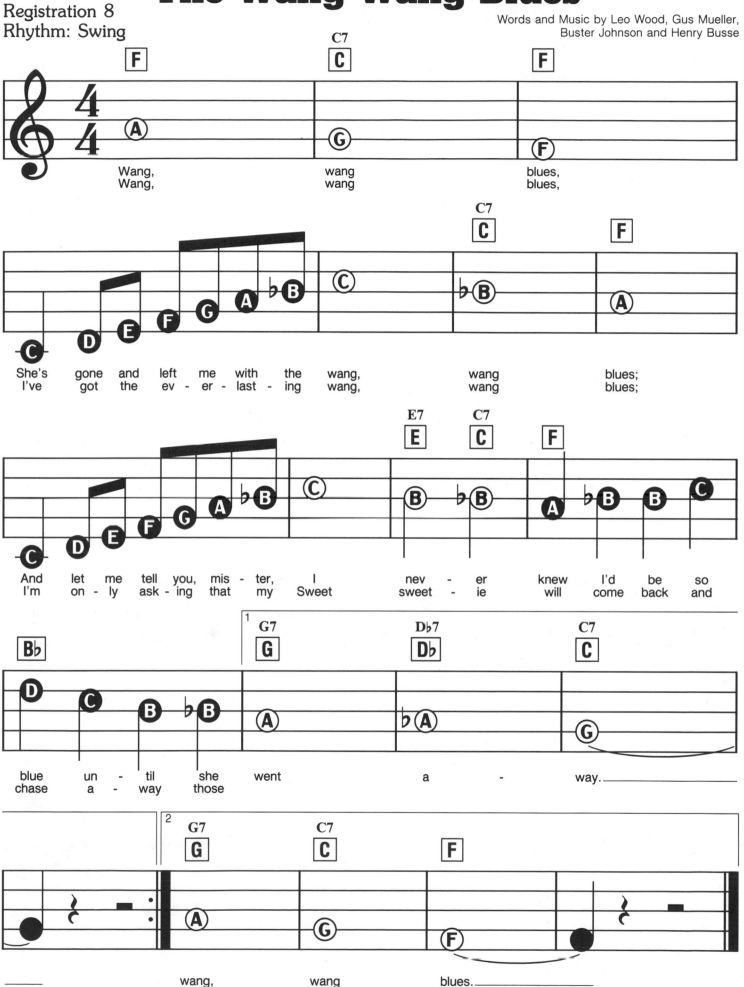

Wang,   wang   blues,
Wang,   wang   blues,

She's gone and left me with the wang,   wang   blues;
I've got the ev - er - last - ing wang,   wang   blues;

And let me tell you, mis - ter, I   nev -   er   knew   I'd be so
I'm on - ly ask - ing that my Sweet   sweet - ie   will   come back so and

blue un - til she went   a - way.
chase a - way those she

wang,   wang   blues.

Sugar Blues

Registration 3
Rhythm: Swing or Fox Trot

Words by Lucy Fletcher
Music by Clarence Williams

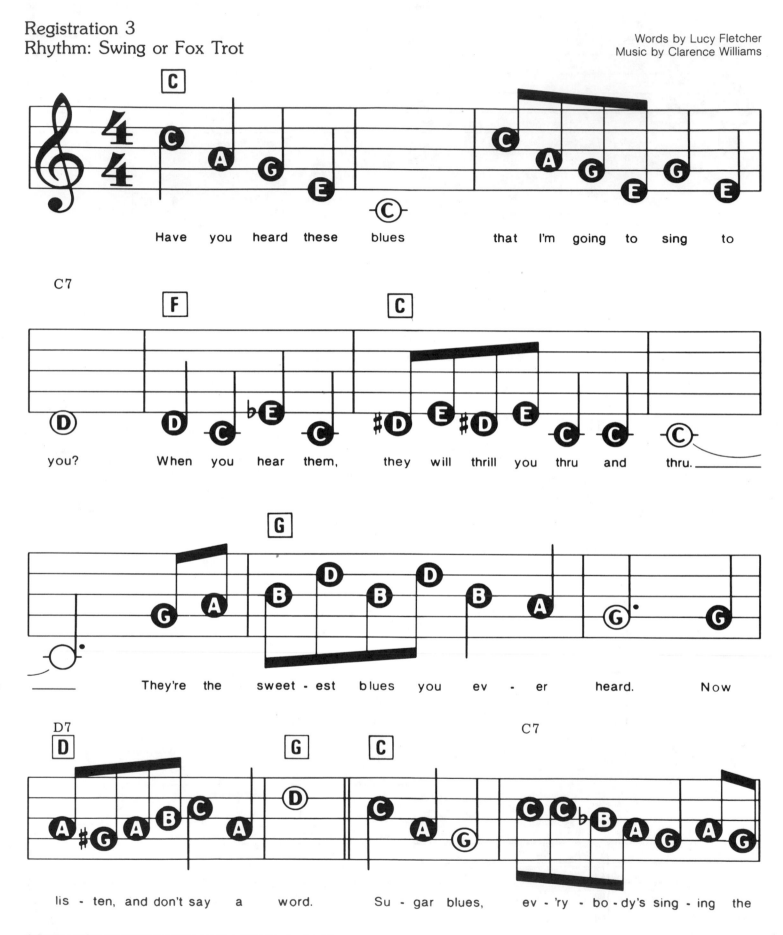

MCA MUSIC PUBLISHING

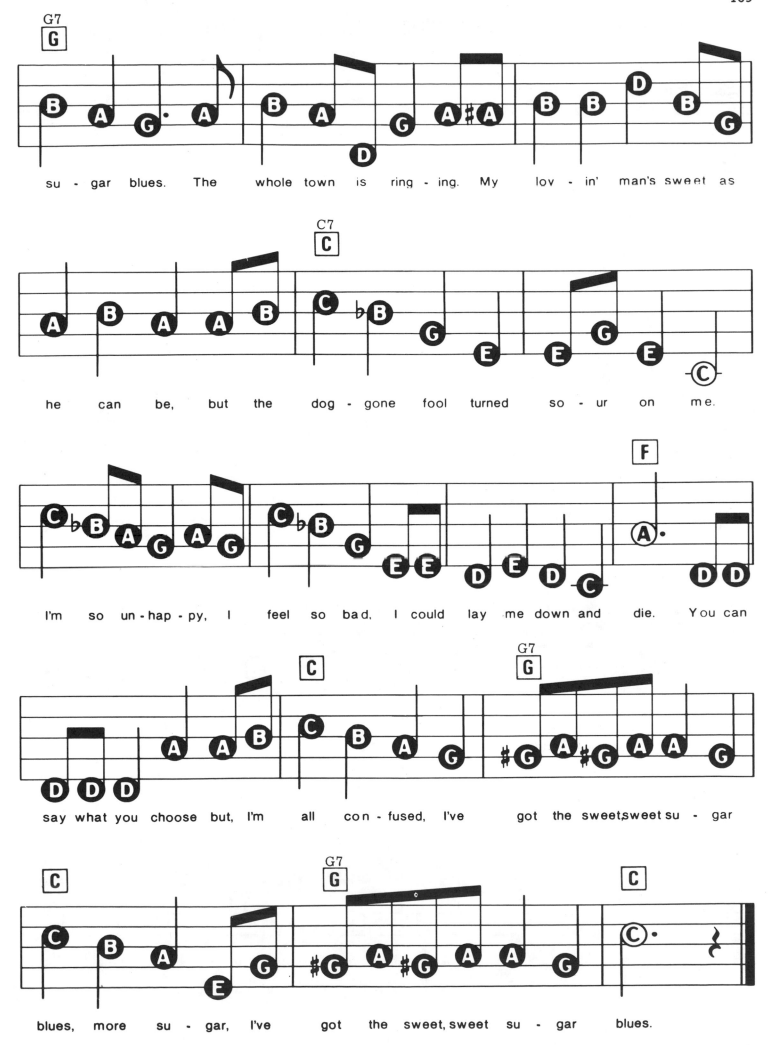

There'll Be Some Changes Made

Registration 7
Rhythm: Swing or Jazz

Words by Billy Higgins
Music by W. Benton Overstreet

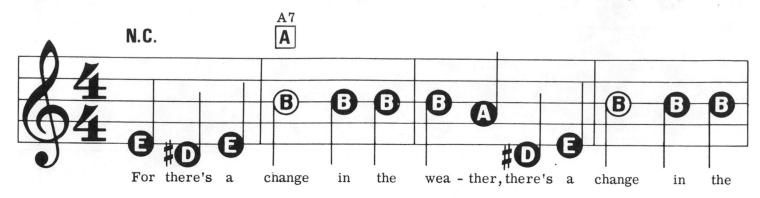

For there's a change in the wea - ther, there's a change in the

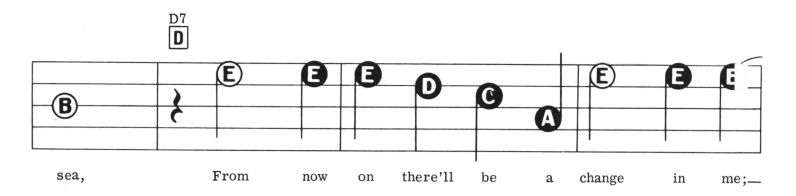

sea, From now on there'll be a change in me;—

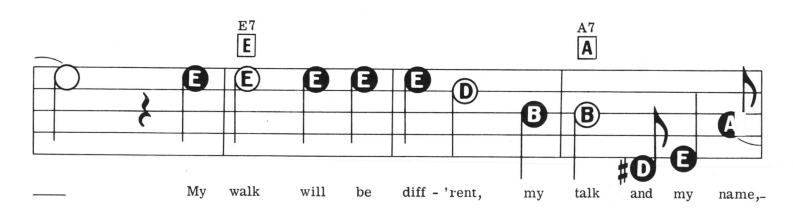

—— My walk will be diff - 'rent, my talk and my name,-

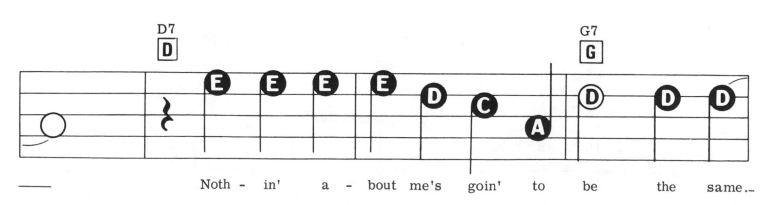

—— Noth - in' a - bout me's goin' to be the same.—

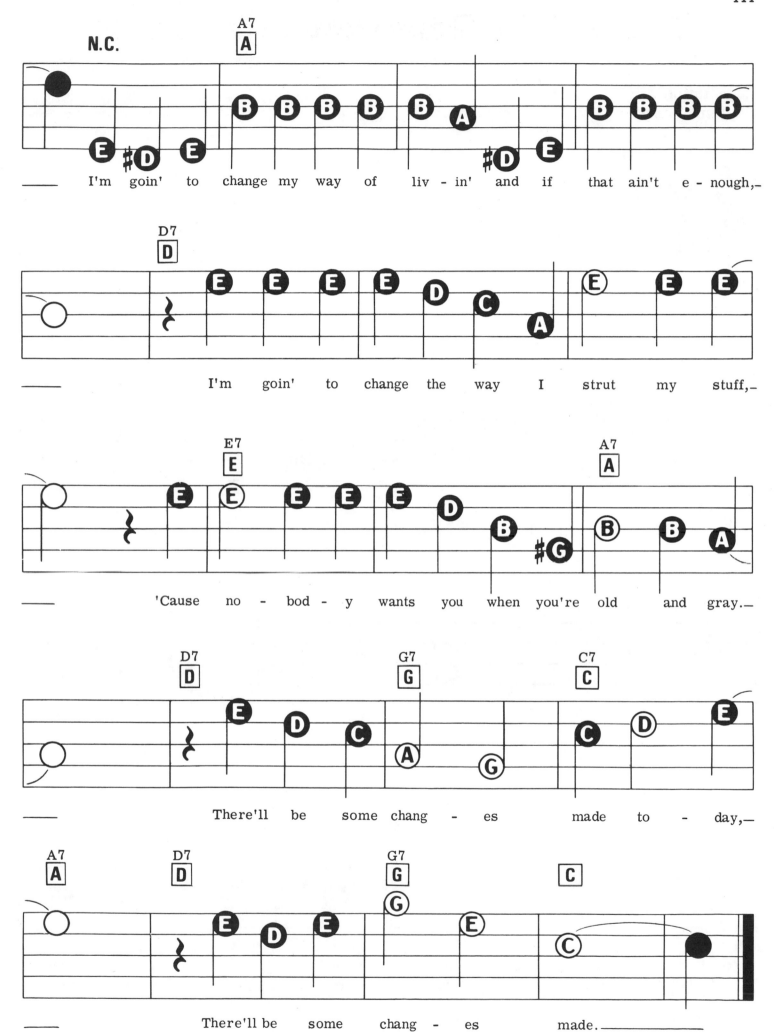

Together

Registration 10
Rhythm: Waltz

Words and Music by B.G. DeSylva,
Ray Henderson & Lew Brown

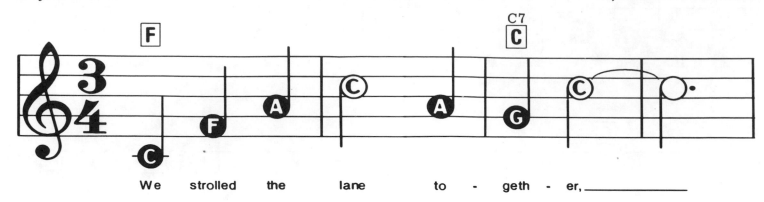

We strolled the lane to - geth - er, _____

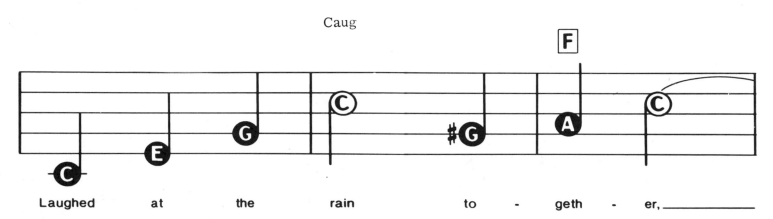

Laughed at the rain to - geth - er, _____

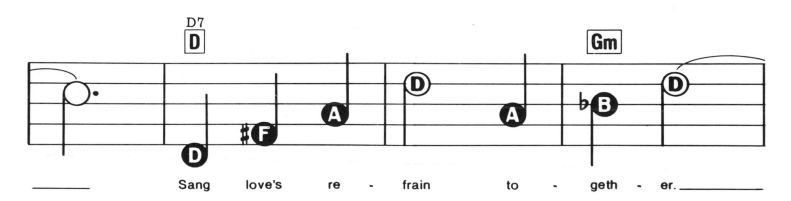

_____ Sang love's re - frain to - geth - er. _____

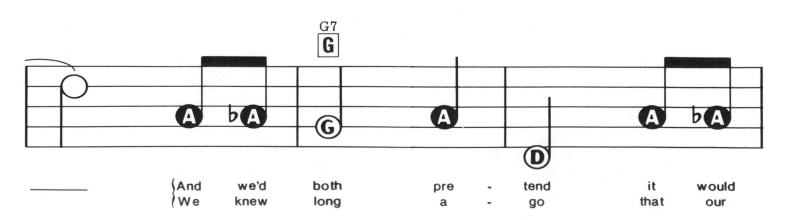

_____ And we'd both pre - tend it would
We knew long a - go that our

The Varsity Drag

(From "GOOD NEWS")

Registration 4
Rhythm: Fox Trot or Swing

Words and Music by B.G. DeSylva
Lew Brown and Ray Henderson

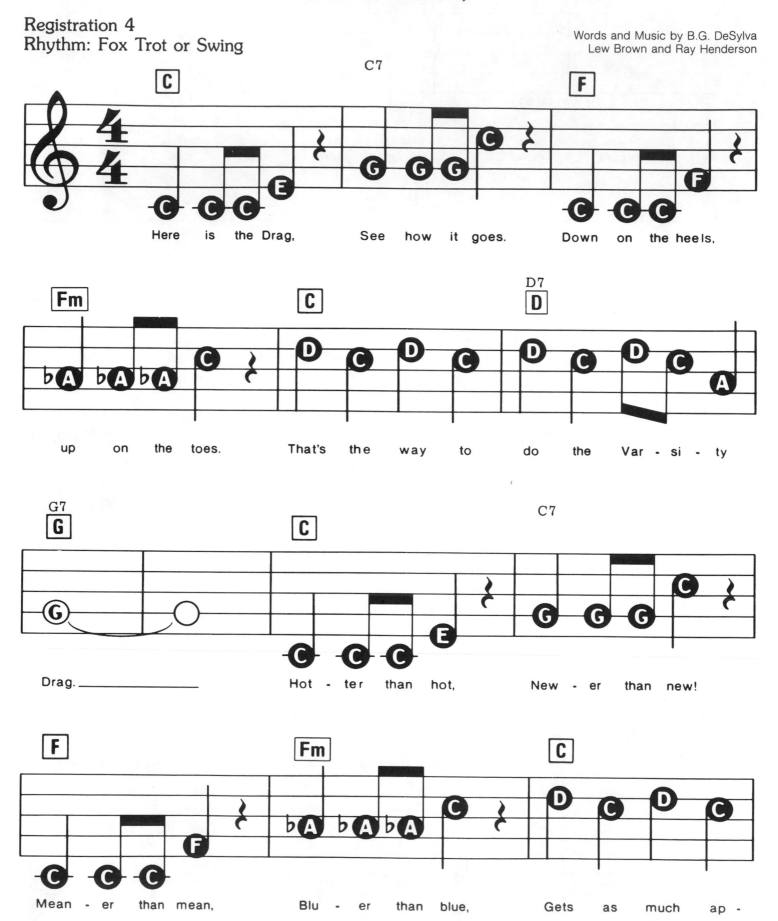

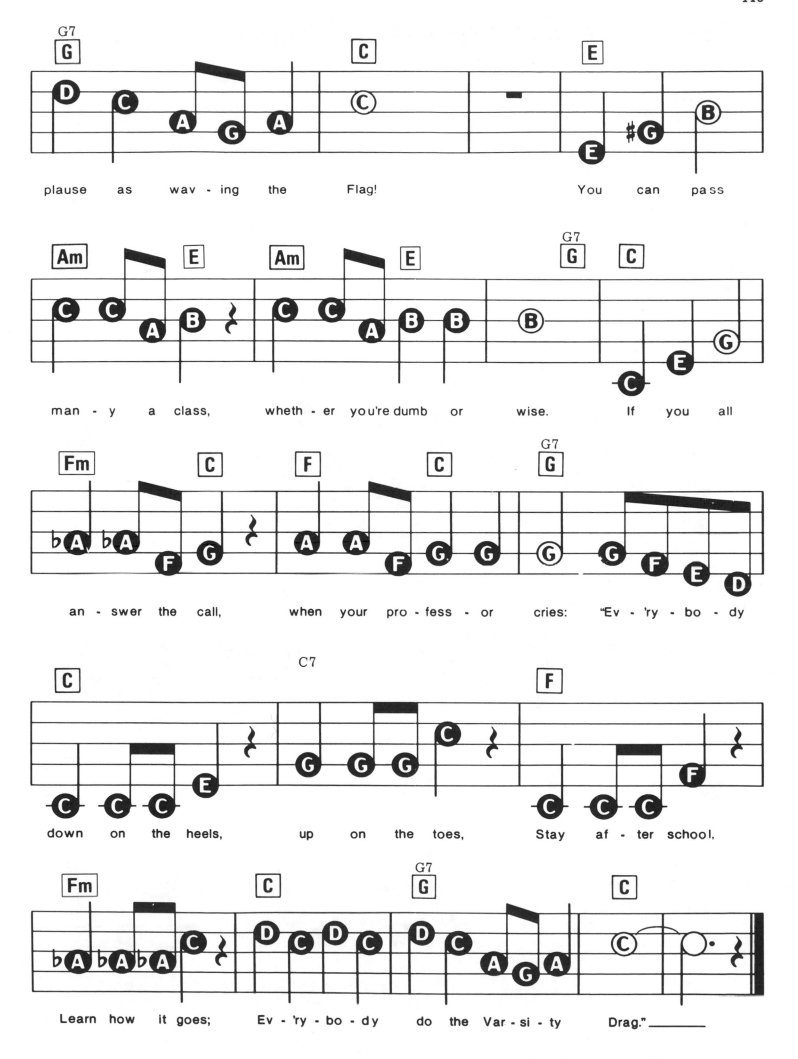

'Way Down Yonder In New Orleans

Registration 7
Rhythm: Swing

By Henry Creamer and J. Turner Layton

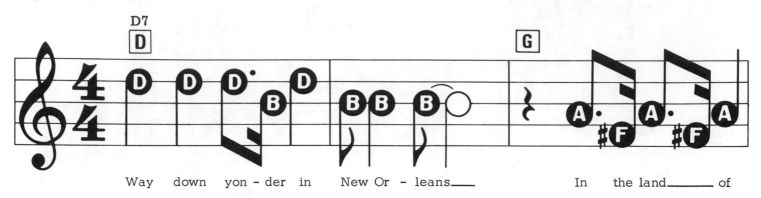

Way down yon-der in New Or - leans___ In the land___ of

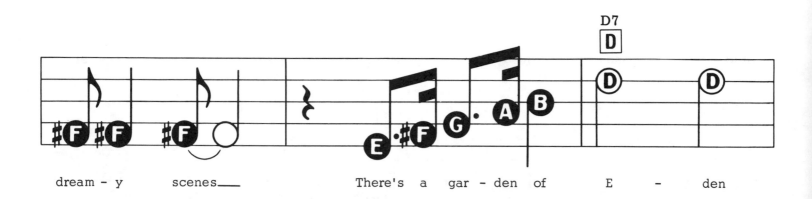

dream - y scenes___ There's a gar - den of E - den

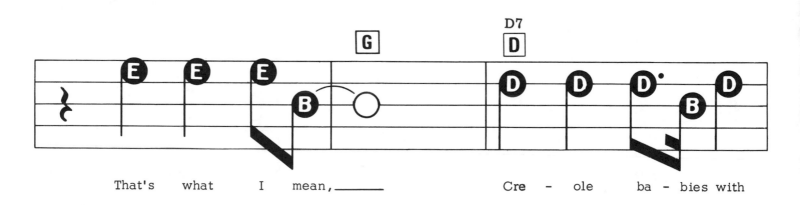

That's what I mean,___ Cre - ole ba - bies with

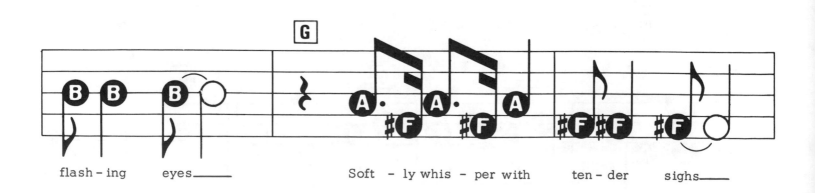

flash - ing eyes___ Soft - ly whis - per with ten - der sighs___

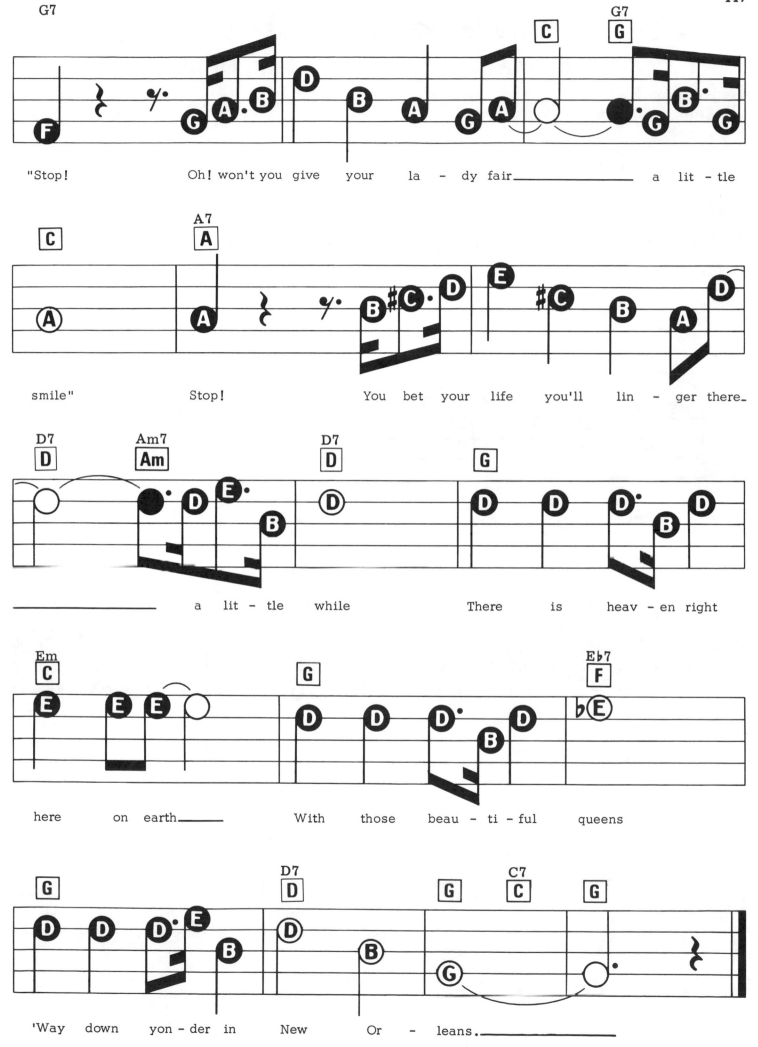

Wedding Bells
(Are Breaking Up That Old Gang Of Mine)

Registration 2
Rhythm: Fox Trot or Swing

Words by Irving Kahal and Willie Raskin
Music by Sammy Fain

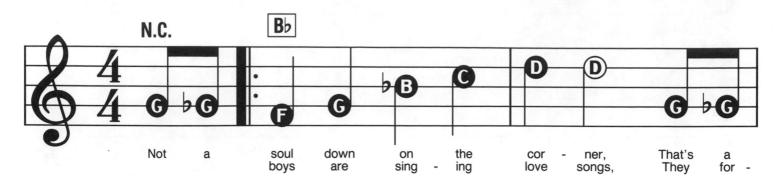

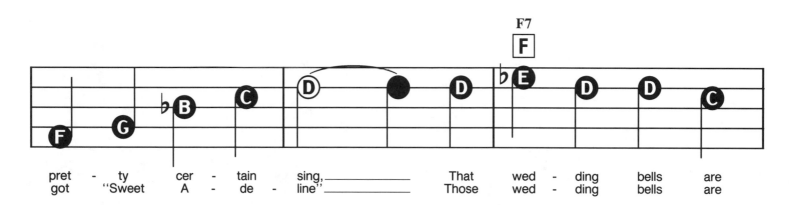

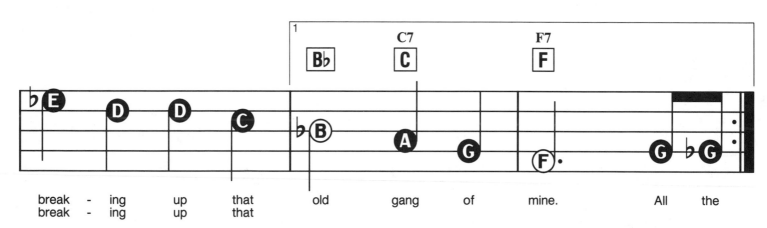

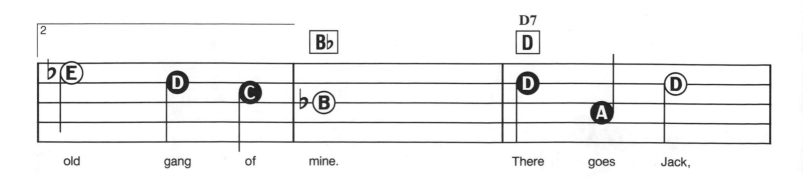

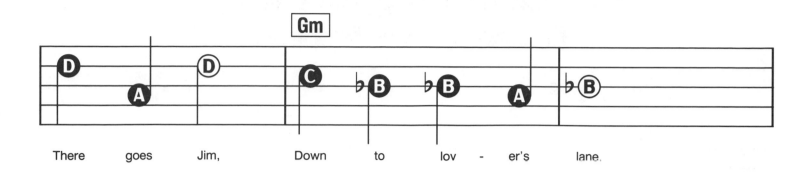

There goes Jim, Down to lov - er's lane.

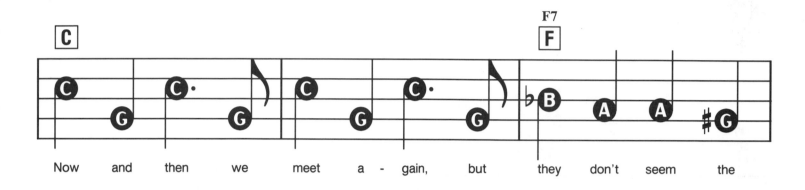

Now and then we meet a - gain, but they don't seem the

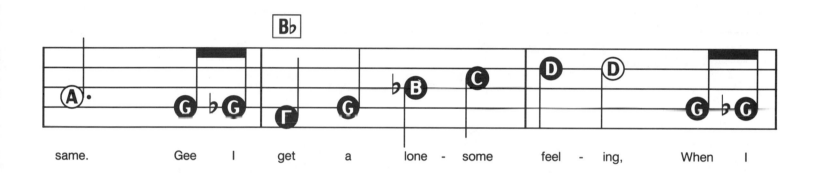

same. Gee I get a lone - some feel - ing, When I

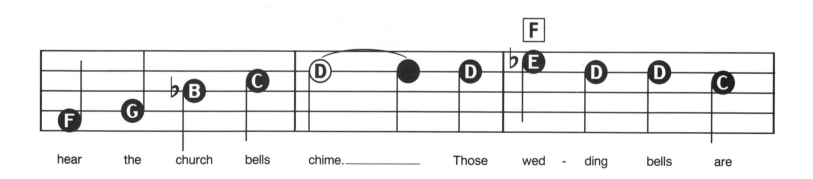

hear the church bells chime._____ Those wed - ding bells are

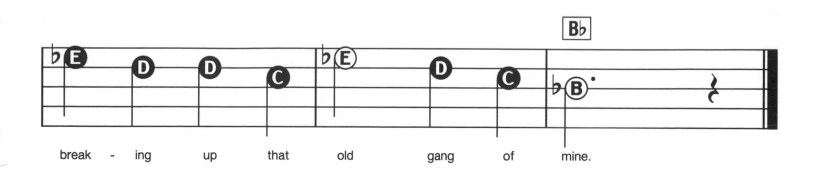

break - ing up that old gang of mine.

When My Sugar Walks Down The Street

Registration 5
Rhythm: Fox Trot or Swing

Words and Music by Gene Austin,
Jimmie McHugh and Irving Mills

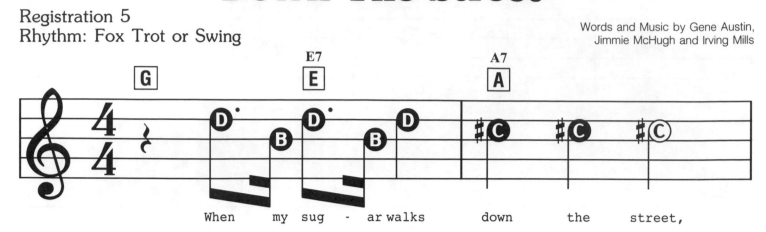

When my sug - ar walks down the street,

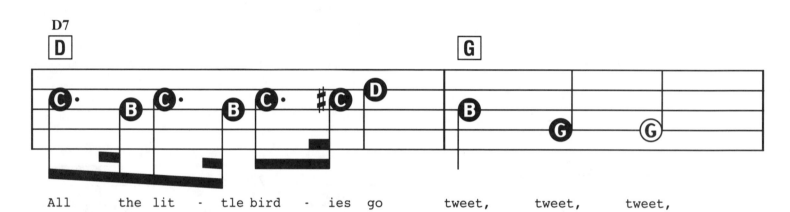

All the lit - tle bird - ies go tweet, tweet, tweet,

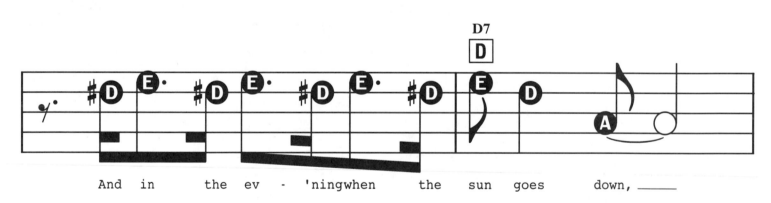

And in the ev - 'ning when the sun goes down, ____

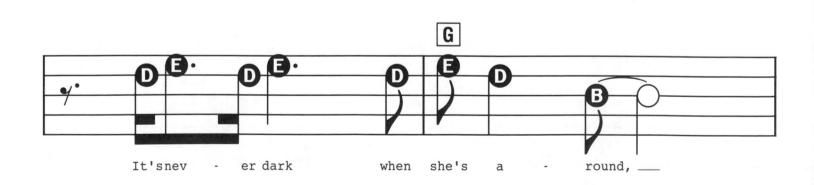

It's nev - er dark when she's a - round, ___

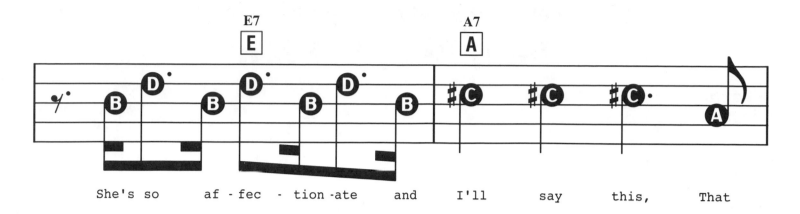

She's so af-fec-tion-ate and I'll say this, That

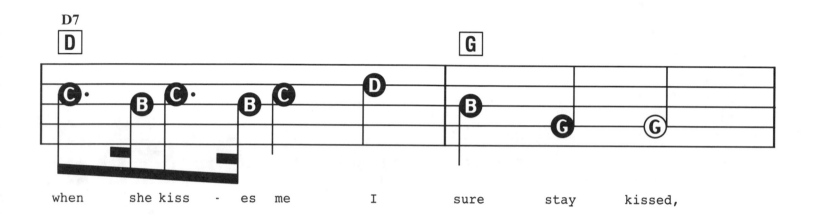

when she kiss - es me I sure stay kissed,

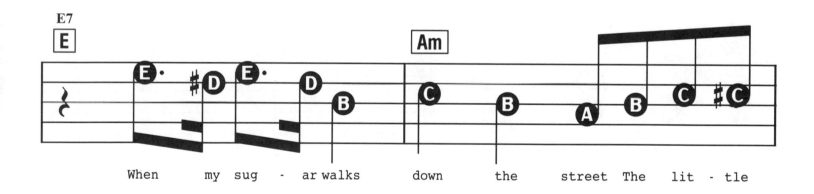

When my sug - ar walks down the street The lit - tle

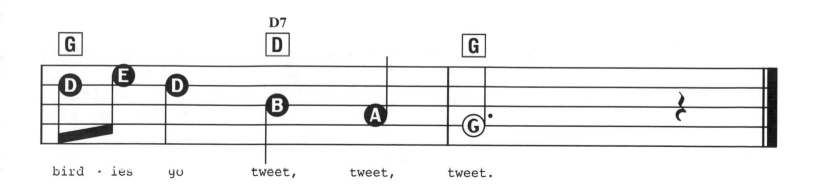

bird - ies go tweet, tweet, tweet.

When The Red, Red Robin Comes Bob, Bob, Bobbin' Along

Registration 5
Rhythm: Fox Trot or Swing

Words and Music by
Harry Woods

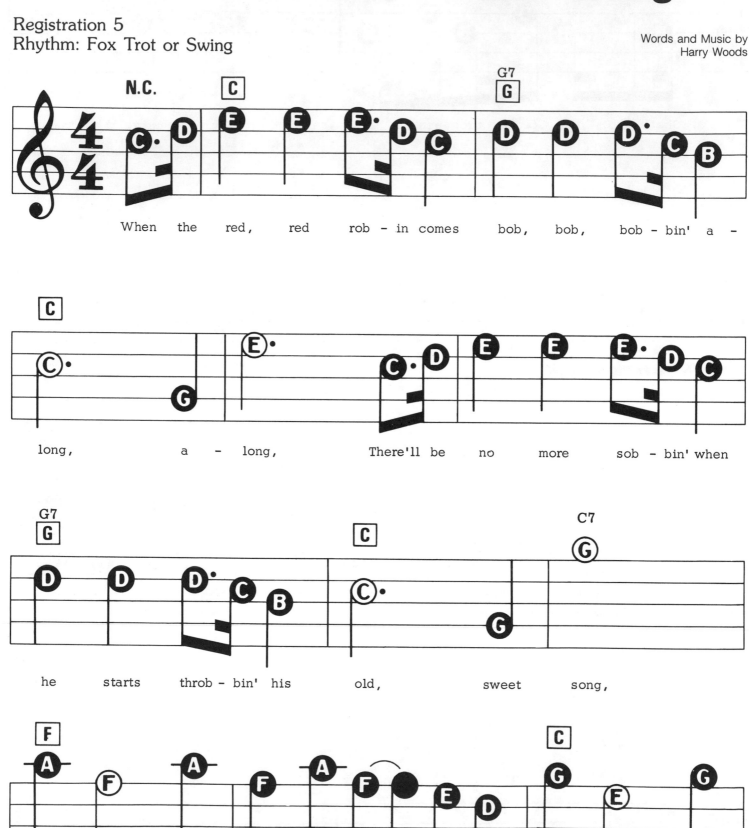

When the red, red rob-in comes bob, bob, bob-bin' a-

long, a - long, There'll be no more sob-bin' when

he starts throb-bin' his old, sweet song,

Wake up, wake up you sleep-y head, Get up, get

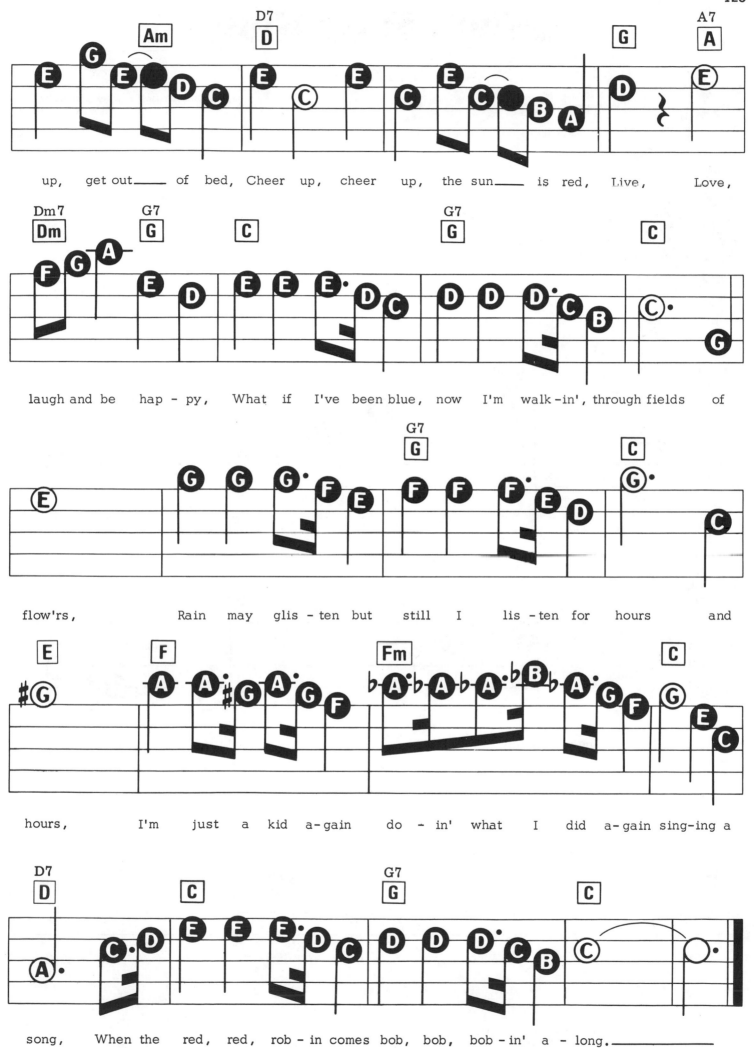

Who's Sorry Now

Registration 1
Rhythm: Fox Trot or Swing

Words by Bert Kalmer and Harry Ruby
Music by Ted Snyder

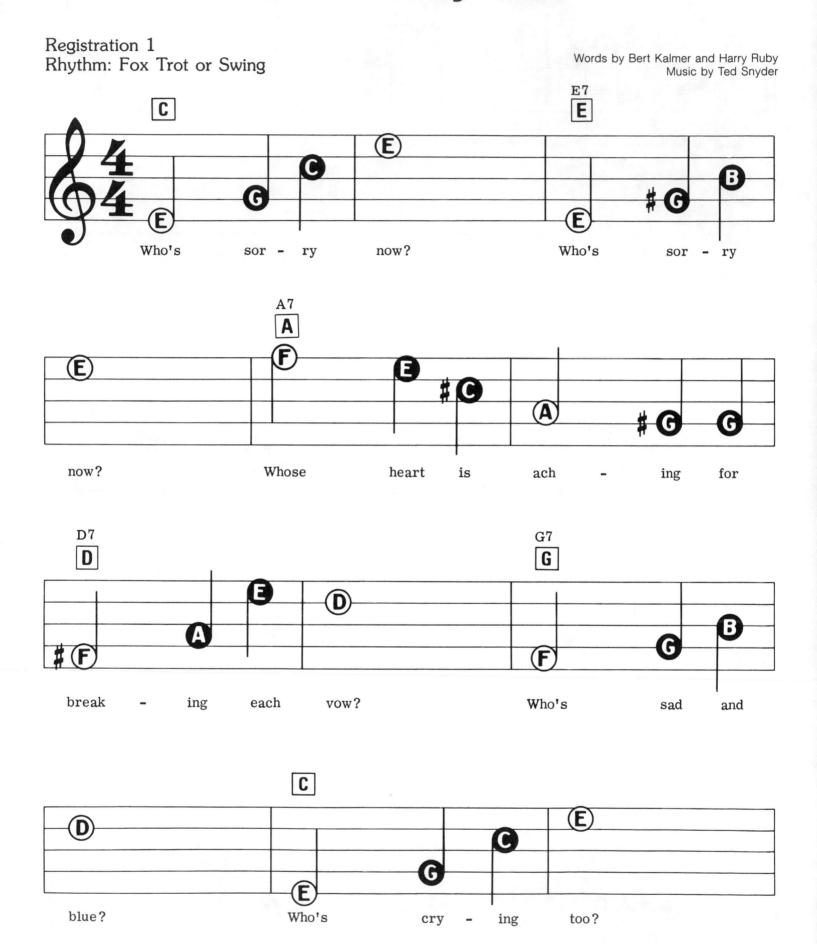

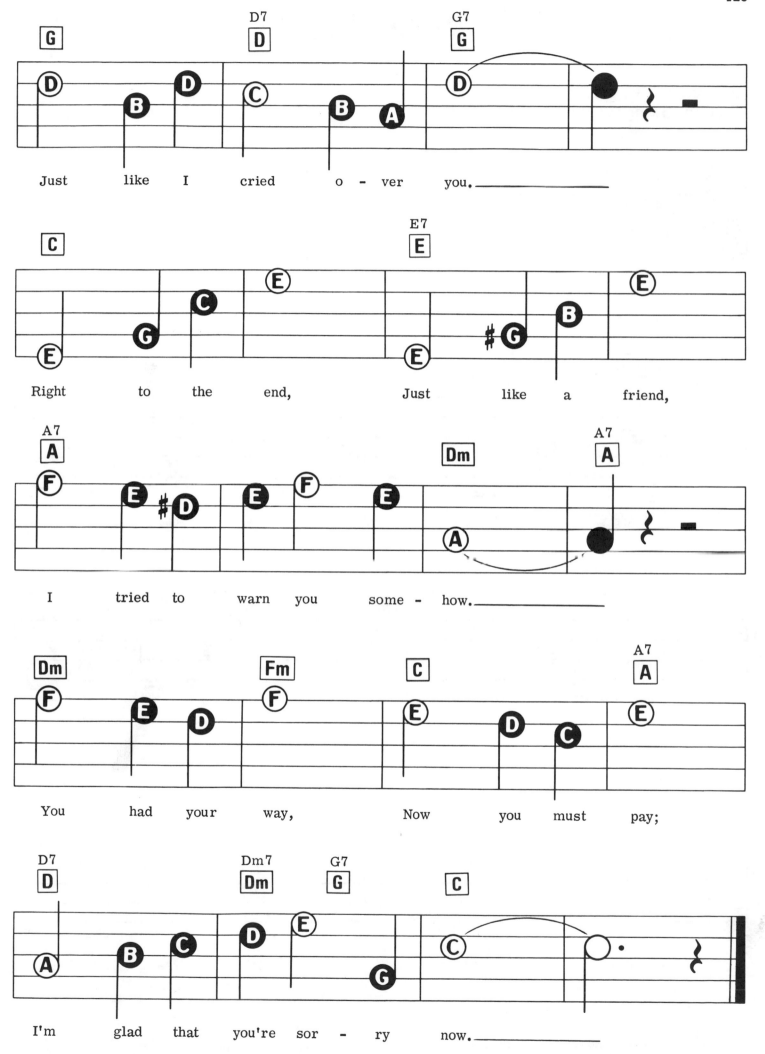

Yearning

Registration 3
Rhythm: Swing

Words and Music by
Benny Davis and Joe Burke

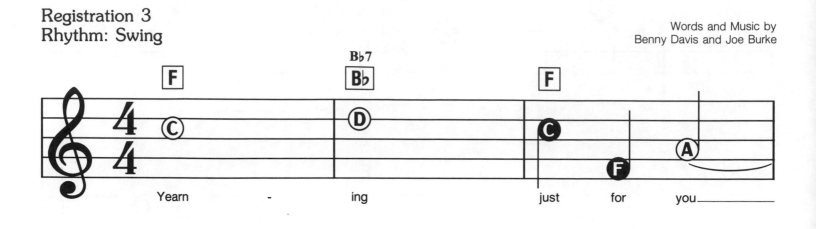

Yearn - ing   just   for   you____

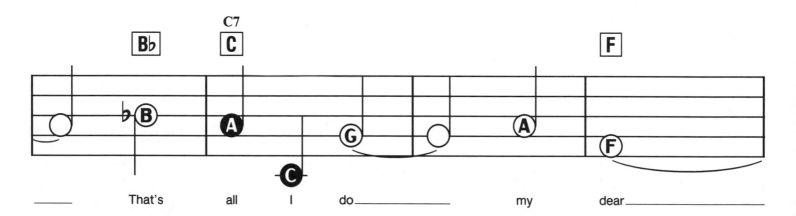

____ That's   all   I   do____   my   dear____

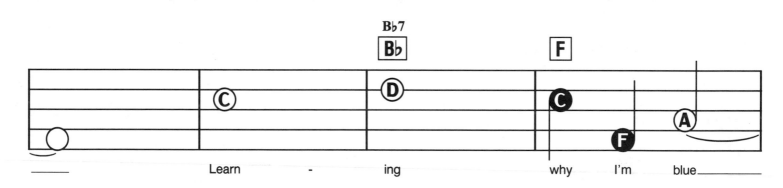

____   Learn - ing   why   I'm   blue____

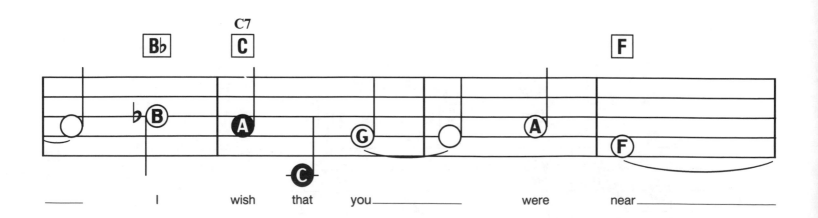

____   I   wish   that   you____   were   near____

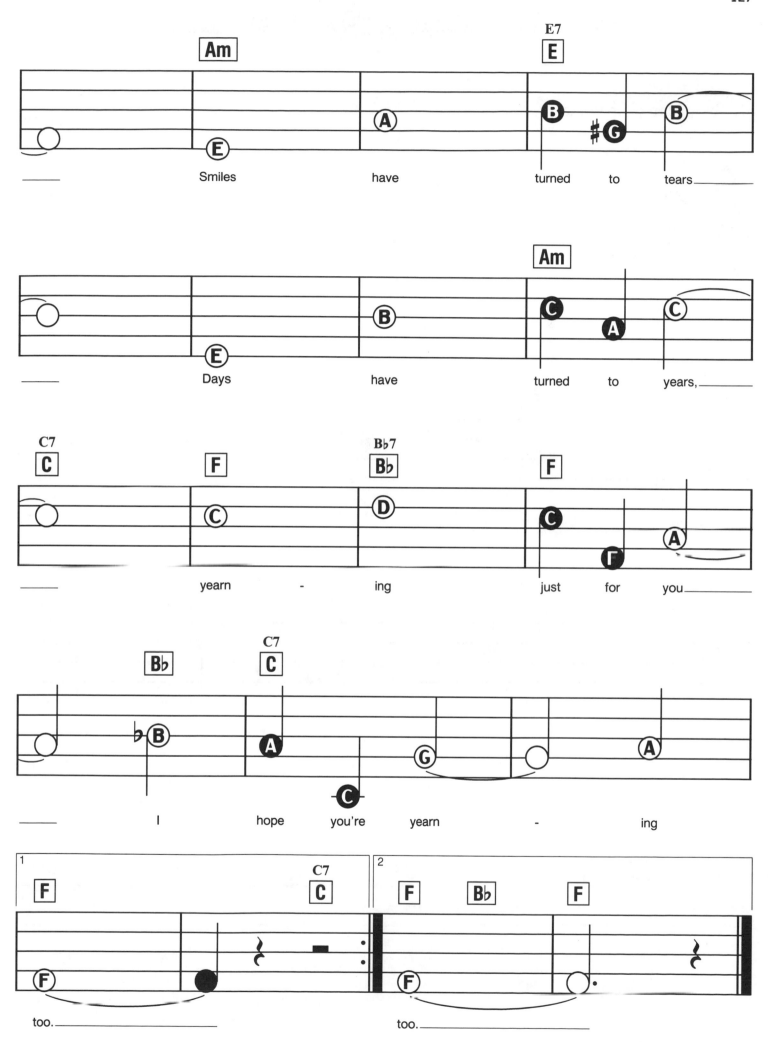

Yes! We Have No Bananas

Registration 5
Rhythm: March or Polka

By Frank Silver and Irving Cohn

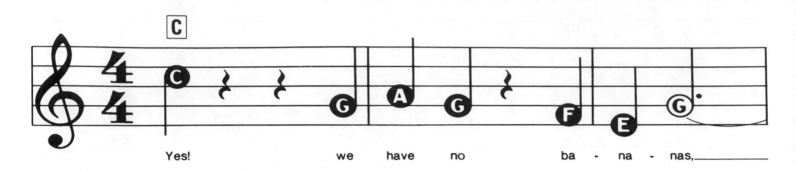

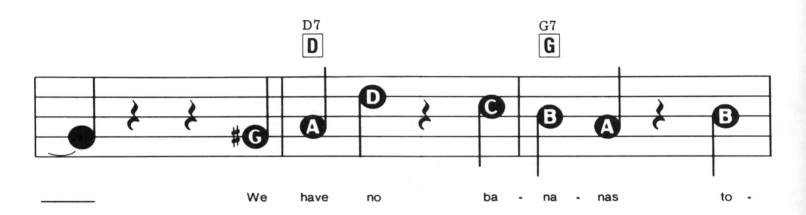

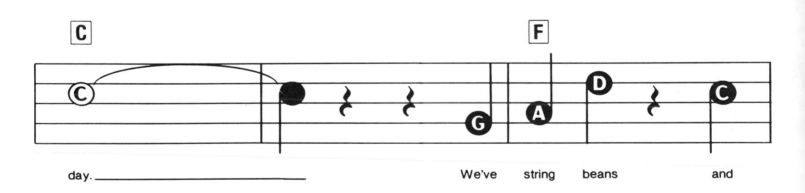

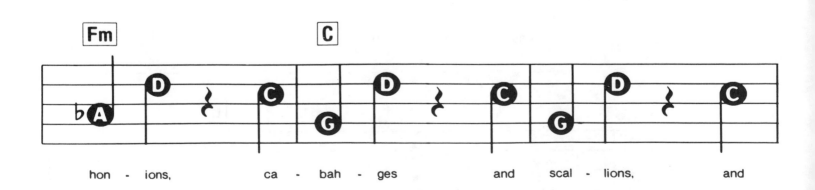

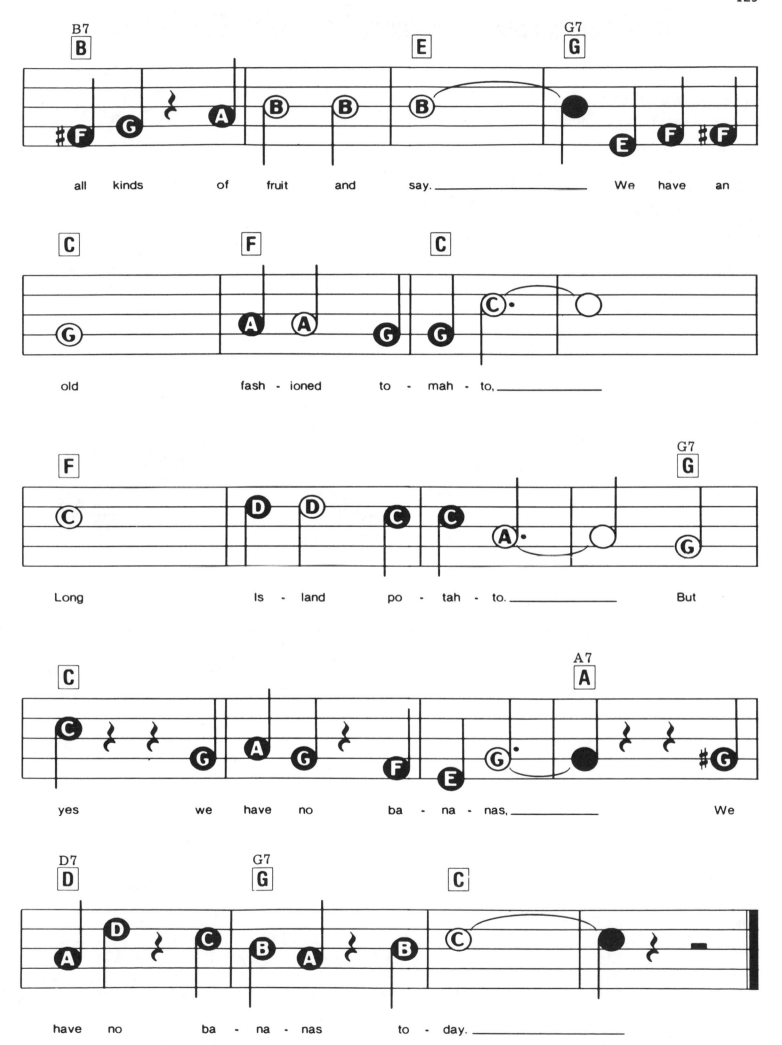

You're The Cream In My Coffee

(From "HOLD EVERYTHING")

Registration 4
Rhythm: Fox Trot or Swing

Words and Music by B.G. DeSylva,
Lew Brown and Ray Henderson

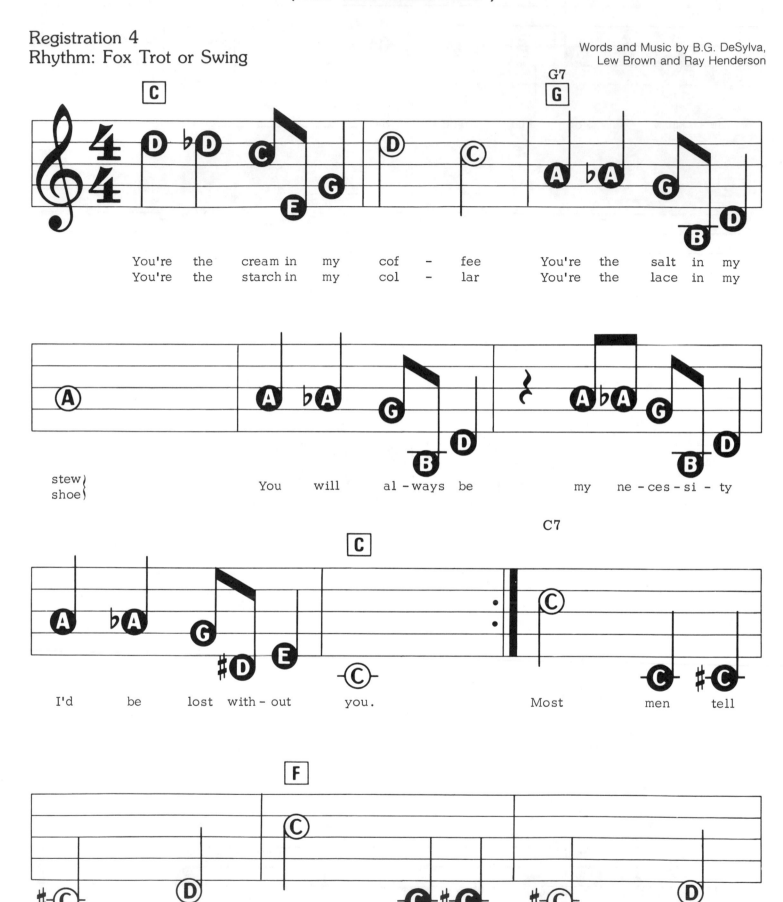

You're the cream in my cof - fee You're the salt in my
You're the starch in my col - lar You're the lace in my

stew)
shoe{   You will al -ways be   my ne -ces -si - ty

I'd be lost with - out you.   Most men tell

love - tales   And   each phrase dove - tails

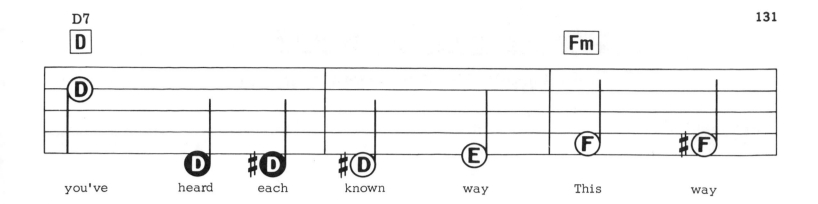

you've heard each known way This way

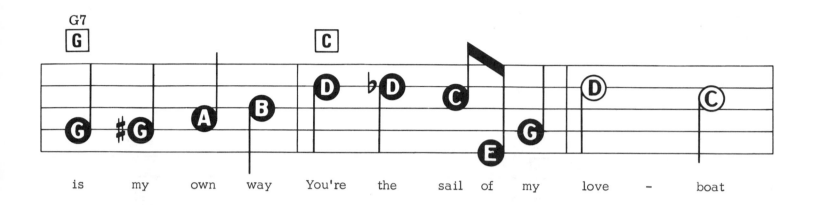

is my own way You're the sail of my love – boat

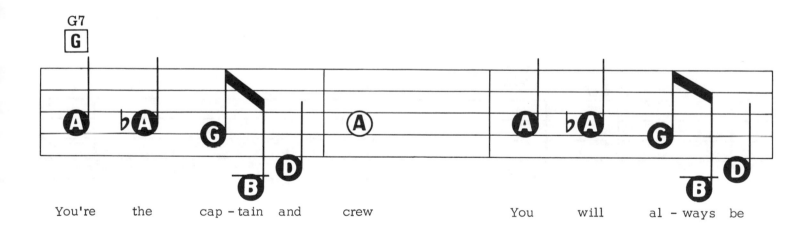

You're the cap-tain and crew You will al-ways be

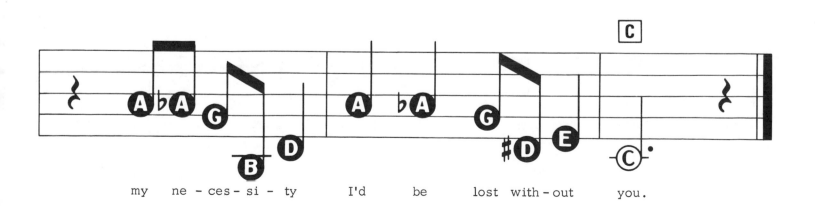

my ne-ces-si-ty I'd be lost with-out you.

When You're Smiling
(The Whole World Smiles With You)

Registration 9
Rhythm: Swing

Words and Music by Mark Fisher,
Joe Goodwin and Larry Shay

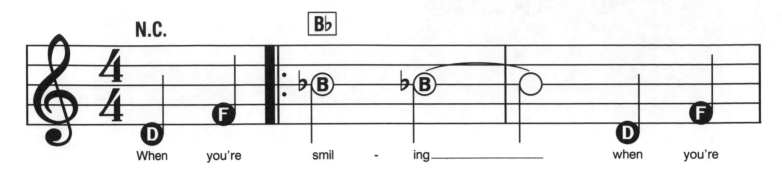

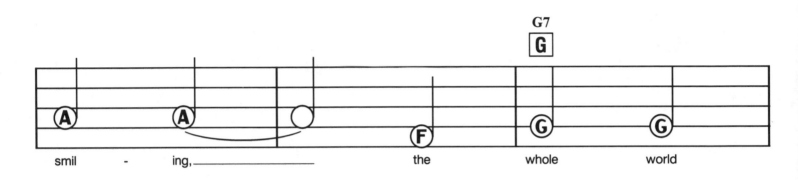

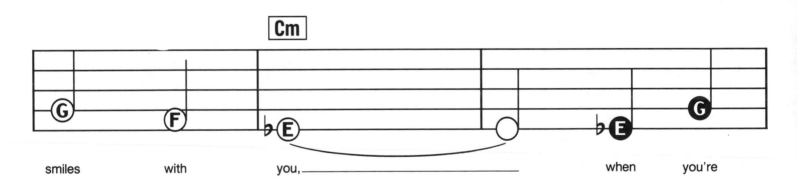

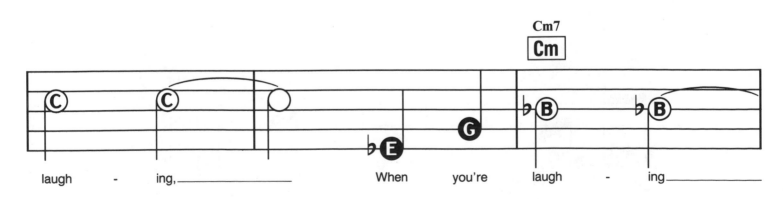

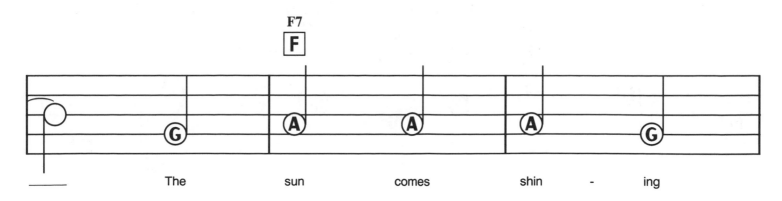

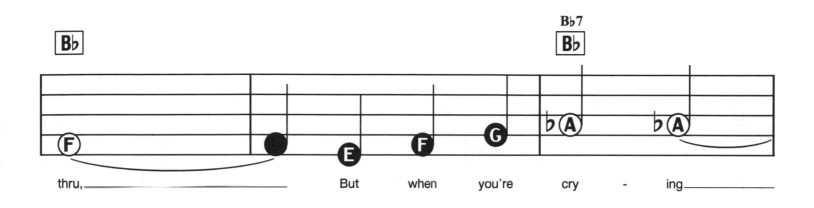

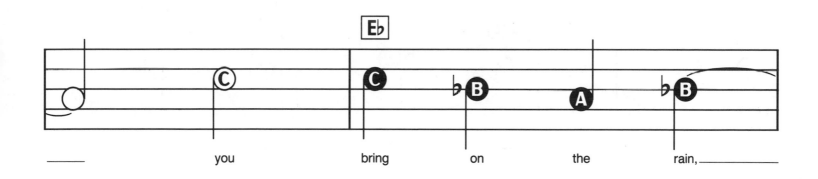

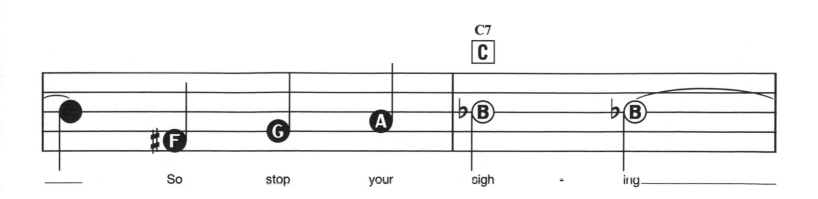

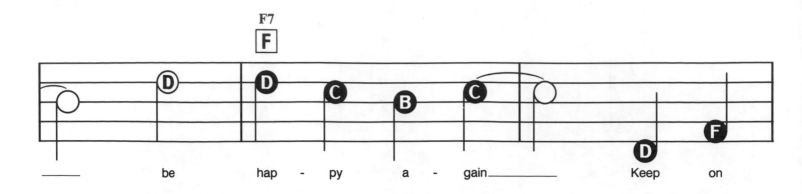

be hap - py a - gain_____ Keep on

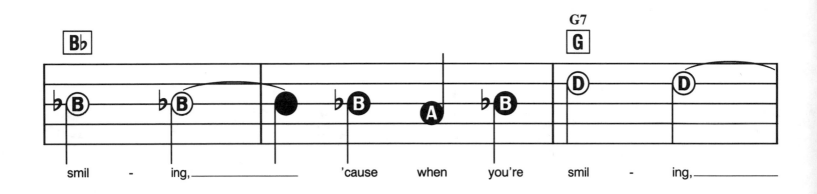

smil - ing,_____ 'cause when you're smil - ing,_____

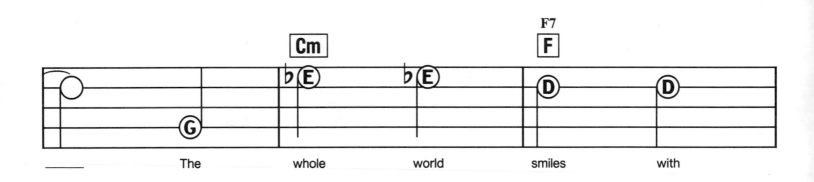

_____ The whole world smiles with

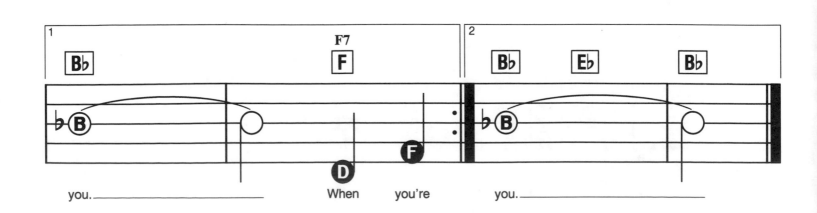

you._____ When you're you._____

E-Z Play® TODAY Registration Guide
For All Organs

On the following chart are 10 numbered registrations for both tonebar (TB) and electronic tab organs. The numbers correspond to the registration numbers on the E-Z Play TODAY songs. Set up as many voices and controls listed for each specific number as you have available on your instrument. For more detailed registrations, ask your dealer for the E-Z Play TODAY Registration Guide for your particular organ model.

REG. NO.		UPPER (SOLO)	LOWER (ACCOMPANIMENT)	PEDAL	GENERALS
1	Tab	Flute 16′, 2′	Diapason 8′ Flute 4′	Flute 16′, 8′	Tremolo/Leslie – Fast
	TB	80 0808 000	(00) 7600 000	46, Sustain	Tremolo/Leslie – Fast (Upper/Lower)
2	Tab	Flute 16′, 8′, 4′, 2′, 1′	Diapason 8′ Flute 8′, 4′	Flute 16′ String 8′	Tremolo/Leslie – Fast
	TB	80 7806 004	(00) 7503 000	46, Sustain	Tremolo/Leslie – Fast (Upper/Lower)
3	Tab	Flute 8′, 4′, 2²/₃′, 2′ String 8′, 4′	Diapason 8′ Flute 4′ String 8′	Flute 16′, 8′	Tremolo/Leslie – Fast
	TB	40 4555 554	(00) 7503 333	46, Sustain	Tremolo/Leslie – Fast (Upper/Lower)
4	Tab	Flute 16′, 8′, 4′ Reed 16′, 8′	Flute 8′, (4) Reed 8′	Flute 8′ String 8′	Tremolo/Leslie – Fast
	TB	80 7766 008	(00) 7540 000	54, Sustain	Tremolo/Leslie – Fast (Upper/Lower)
5	Tab	Flute 16′, 4′, 2′ Reed 16′, 8′ String 8′, 4′	Diapason 8′ Reed 8′ String 4′	Flute 16′, 8′ String 8′	Tremolo/Leslie
	TB	40 4555 554 Add all 4′, 2′ voices	(00) 7503 333	57, Sustain	
6	Tab	Flute 16′, 8′, 4′ Diapason 8′ String 8′	Diapason 8′ Flute 8′ String 4′	Diapason 8′ Flute 8′	Tremolo/Leslie – Slow (Chorale)
	TB	45 6777 643	(00) 6604 020	64, Sustain	Tremolo/Leslie – Slow (Chorale)
7	Tab	Flute 16′, 8′, 5¹/₃′, 2²/₃′, 1′	Flute 8′, 4′ Reed 8′	Flute 8′ String 8′	Chorus (optional) Perc Attack
	TB	88 0088 000	(00) 4333 000	45, Sustain	Tremolo/Leslie – Slow (Chorale)
8	Tab	Piano Preset or Flute 8′ or Diapason 8′	Diapason 8′	Flute 8′	
	TB	00 8421 000	(00) 4302 010	43, Sustain	Perc Piano
9	Tab	Clarinet Preset or Flute 8′ Reed 16′, 8′	Flute 8′ Reed 8′	Flute 16′, 8′	Vibrato
	TB	00 8080 840	(00) 5442 000	43, Sustain	Vibrato
10	Tab	String (Violin) Preset or Flute 16′ String 8′, 4′	Flute 8′ Reed 8′	Flute 16′, 8′	Vibrato or Delayed Vibrato
	TB	00 7888 888	(00) 7765 443	57, Sustain	Vibrato or Delayed Vibrato

NOTE: TIBIAS may be used in place of FLUTES. VIBRATO may be used in place of LESLIE.